WRITING A POEM

WRITING A POEM

By
Florence Trefethen

12816

Publishers   THE WRITER, INC.   Boston

Library of Congress Catalog Card Number: 75–110496
International Standard Book Number: 0–87116–013–7

MANUFACTURED IN THE UNITED STATES OF AMERICA

ACKNOWLEDGMENTS

"A Civil Servant." Copyright © 1955 by Robert Graves. From *Collected Poems of 1955*, Doubleday & Co. Reprinted by permission of Collins-Knowlton-Wing, Inc.

"A High-Toned Old Christian Woman." Copyright © 1923 and renewed 1951 by Wallace Stevens. Reprinted from *Collected Poems of Wallace Stevens*, by permission of Alfred A. Knopf, Inc.

"A Kiss." From *Collected Poems* by Henry Austin Dobson, Dodd, Mead & Company. Reprinted by permission of Dodd, Mead & Company.

"A Weaver of Carpets." Reprinted with the permission of the author, Sam Toperoff. Copyright © 1966 by The Atlantic Monthly Company, Boston, Mass. Reprinted with permission.

"American Primitive." Copyright © 1954 by William Jay Smith. Reprinted by permission of William Jay Smith.

"Apfel." By Reinhard Döhl. From *An Anthology of Concrete Poetry*, edited by Emmett Williams. Copyright © 1967 by Something Else Press, Inc., New York. All rights reserved. Reprinted by permission of Something Else Press, Inc.

"Ars Poetica." From *Collected Poems 1917–1952*, by Archibald MacLeish, Houghton Mifflin Company. Reprinted with the permission of the Houghton Mifflin Company.

"Coup de Grâce." From *Collected Poems: 1930–1965*, by A. D. Hope. Copyright © 1960, 1962 by A. D. Hope. Copyright 1963, 1966 in all countries of the International Copyright Union. All rights reserved. Reprinted by permission of The Viking Press, Inc.

"Deciduous Branch." Copyright © 1929, 1930, 1944, 1951, 1953, 1954, 1956, 1957, 1958 by Stanley Kunitz. From *Selected Poems 1928–1958*, by Stanley Kunitz, by permission of Atlantic-Little, Brown and Co.

"Design." From *The Poetry of Robert Frost*, edited by Edward Connery Lathem. Copyright © 1936 by Robert Frost. Copyright © 1964 by Lesley Frost Ballantine. Reprinted by permission of Holt, Rinehart and Winston, Inc.

"Do not go gentle into that good night." Dylan Thomas, *Collected Poems*. Copyright © 1952 by Dylan Thomas. Reprinted by permission of New Directions Publishing Corporation.

"Eight O'Clock." From *The Collected Poems of A. E. Housman*. Copyright © 1922 by Holt, Rinehart and Winston, Inc. Copyright © 1950 by Barclays Bank Ltd. Reprinted by permission of Holt, Rinehart and Winston, Inc.

"Eighth Air Force." Reprinted with the permission of Farrar, Straus & Giroux, Inc. from *The Complete Poems*, by Randall Jarrell. Copyright © 1947, 1969 by Mrs. Randall Jarrell.

"fowl, flap, swing, wing," etc. Special permission granted by *Read* magazine, published by American Education Publications/A Xerox Company, Columbus, Ohio.

haiku. By Eva Gorham Craig and Gustave Keyser. Reprinted by permission of *American Haiku,* Platteville, Wisconsin.

"Hallalujah: A Sestina." Copyright © 1960 by Robert Francis. Reprinted from *The Orb Weaver,* by permission of Wesleyan University Press. Robert Francis's remarks about the poem reprinted from *Poet's Choice,* edited by Paul Engle and Joseph Langland, with the permission of The Dial Press.

"In White." Original version of "Design" from *The Dimensions of Robert Frost,* by Reginald L. Cook. Copyright © 1958 by Reginald L. Cook. Reprinted by permission of Holt, Rinehart and Winston, Inc. Also reprinted with the permission of the Huntington Library, San Marino, California, from HM25361, a letter from Robert Frost to Susan H. Ward, January 15, 1912.

"Lately, at Night." From *The Privilege,* by Maxine Kumin. Copyright © 1964 by Maxine Kumin. Reprinted by permission of Harper & Row, Publishers, Inc.

"Mushrooms." Copyright © 1960 by Sylvia Plath. Reprinted from *The Colossus and Other Poems,* by Sylvia Plath, by permission of Alfred A. Knopf, Inc.

"Nude Descending a Staircase," From *Nude Descending A Staircase,* by X. J. Kennedy, Doubleday & Company, Inc. Copyright © 1956, 1958, 1959, 1960, 1961 by X. J. Kennedy. Reprinted by permission of X. J. Kennedy.

"On Seeing Weather-Beaten Trees." From *Verse,* by Adelaide Crapsey. Copyright © 1922 and renewed 1950 by The Adelaide Crapsey Foundation. Reprinted by permission of Alfred A. Knopf, Inc.

"Piazza Piece." Copyright © 1927 and renewed 1966 by John Crowe Ransom. Reprinted from *Selected Poems,* by John Crowe Ransom, by permission of Alfred A. Knopf, Inc.

"Pied Beauty." From *Poems of Gerard Manley Hopkins,* published by the Oxford University Press.

"Pigeon Woman" (Copyright © 1962 May Swenson), which first appeared in *The New Yorker,* is reprinted with the permission of Charles Scribner's Sons from *To Mix with Time,* by May Swenson.

"Ruminants." Printed by permission of The Society of Authors (London) as the literary representative of the Estate of James Joyce.

"Said Agatha Christie." From "Seven Double Dactyls." Reprinted with the permission of the author, George Starbuck. Copyright © 1969 by The Atlantic Monthly Company, Boston, Mass. Reprinted with permission.

"Sailing to Byzantium." Reprinted with permission of The Macmillan Company from *The Collected Poems of William Butler Yeats.* Copyright © 1928 by The Macmillan Company, renewed 1956 by Georgie Yeats.

Sky and Water. By M. C. Escher, from the collection of C. V. S. Roosevelt, Washington, D.C. Reproduced with the permission of M. C. Escher and C. V. S. Roosevelt.

"stay in line." Printed with the permission of the author, Jane Poston.

"The Descent." William Carlos Williams, *Pictures from Brueghel*. Copyright © 1948 by William Carlos Williams. Reprinted by permission of New Directions Publishing Corporation.

"THE LATE ASTRONAUT IN THE BOSTON GLOBE." From *The Marriage Wig*, copyright © 1968 by Ruth Whitman. Reprinted by permission of Harcourt, Brace & World, Inc. Earlier version and critique printed by permission of Ruth Whitman.

"The Map-Maker on His Art." Reprinted from *Mirrors & Windows: Poems*, by Howard Nemerov by permission of The University of Chicago Press. Copyright © 1958 by Howard Nemerov.

"The Pardon." From *Ceremony and Other Poems*, copyright, © 1948, 1949, 1950, by Richard Wilbur. Reprinted by permission of Harcourt, Brace & World, Inc.

"The Rest." Ezra Pound, *Personae*. Copyright © 1926 by Ezra Pound. Reprinted by permission of New Directions Publishing Corporation.

"The Soul selects her own Society." Reprinted by permission of the publishers and the Trustees of Amherst College from Thomas H. Johnson, Editor, *The Poems of Emily Dickinson*, Cambridge, Mass.: The Belknap Press of Harvard University Press, Copyright © 1951, 1955, by The President and Fellows of Harvard College.

"Tilly." From *Collected Poems* by James Joyce. Copyright © 1927 by James Joyce. All rights reserved. Reprinted by permission of The Viking Press, Inc.

"To a Steam Roller." Reprinted with permission of The Macmillan Company from *The Complete Poems of Marianne Moore*. Copyright © 1935 by Marianne Moore, renewed 1963 by Marianne Moore & T. S. Eliot.

"To the Snake." Denise Levertov, *With Eyes at the Back of Our Heads*. Copyright © 1958 by Denise Levertov Goodman. "To the Snake" was first printed in *Poetry*. Reprinted by permission of New Directions Publishing Corporation.

"un." Copyright © 1938 by E. E. Cummings; renewed, 1966, by Marion Morehouse Cummings. Reprinted from *Poems 1923–1954*, by E. E. Cummings, by permission of Harcourt, Brace & World, Inc.

"Upon a Spider Catching a Fly." From *The Poetical Works of Edward Taylor*, ed. by Thomas H. Johnson (Princeton Paperback, 1966). Copyright © Rockland 1939; Princeton University Press, 1943. Reprinted by permission of Princeton University Press.

CONTENTS

FOREWORD

Books that set out to give advice about writing anything, especially poetry, need to begin with an apology. No program of instruction can promise to produce a good poem, even from a writer who is imaginative, intelligent, and industrious. The number of variables that come together for making a poem— the subject, the writer's grasp of that subject, the discovery of words and forms to express it, temperament, intuitions about feeling and language, judgment, and many more—resist being reduced to a step-by-step method designed to assure a successful result.

What, then, can this book do to justify its place on the desk of the motivated but relatively inexperienced amateur poet? It will describe the progressive stages that go into the making of most competent poems—planning, the actual work with language and form, appraisal and revision—and point towards some of the problems that writers can encounter in these stages. By presenting alternatives in technique, it may widen a writer's view of what he can attempt. The Journal Projects appended to each section except the last are organized to encourage practice with those elements of craftsmanship that contribute to making competent poems. And the book includes as illustrations works that have admirably succeeded in achieving the goal of most poems—making the link between the shaping imagination of the poet and the receptive consciousness of the reader.

Among the many who feel the impulse to write poems, either sporadically or all the time, this book will be most useful for those who combine three qualities. First, an enjoyment of words, their meanings, their histories, their arrangement and manipulation; in short, a delight in the English language. Second, a flexible point of view about what is acceptable as poetry, a willingness to entertain the notion that poetry can take various subjects, forms, and modes, and that this diversity is part of what makes poetry exciting. Third, an appreciation of the energy and self-critical persistence that are needed to make a poem, and the intention to do some hard work. If someone who reads this book is also endowed with acute powers of observation, creative imagination, an empathic view of the world, and a talent for using words so that others understand him, he begins with the equipment needed for writing memorable poetry.

The beginning poet who works through the sections that follow ought to have at his side a good general dictionary, a thesaurus, and a rhyming dictionary. All of these can be invaluable assistants. He will also need a thick journal in which to work on the Projects, a loose-leaf book if he is instinctively a hoarder of notes, otherwise a bound book that will compel such hoarding. In writing poetry, the work sheets—false starts, ideas that seem to wither before they grow, forms that resist completion, alternate lines and phrases—should never be discarded, no matter how poor and unpromising they look; they may later prove to be the nucleus of something splendid. It is useful to date every page of work, whether its contents are rough notes or finished lines.

This book begins gently, and the early Journal Projects are relatively easy. As the reader becomes adjusted to the process of planning a poem and accumulates some confidence about writing, he will be exposed to increasingly difficult material and Projects, but none so difficult that they need arrest his progress.

The book has been arranged to be traversed without haste so that readers can take time to ponder over the sections and to enjoy working on the Journal Projects. The Projects are in meaningful sequence, but, if any one becomes a barrier to further work or a source of frustration and anxiety, the reader should abandon it, at least temporarily. He is alone with his journal, and no one will presume to criticize any private arrangements he makes to further his own development.

Finally, the working poet can have no better companions than others who share his interest. If he is among colleagues who write poetry, or at least appreciate it, he is unusually fortunate. But even if he works in his own isolated corner surrounded by people who are busy in other ways, he can read the poetry of his contemporaries and of those from the past who have already labored through the stages of writing a poem.

MAKING PLANS

BEGINNING WITH AN IDEA

How do poems begin? In many, various ways. Something the poet sees or hears may light up a corner of his mind, illuminating associations that need to be stated in poetry. Or he may experience feelings that compel concrete poetic expression either immediately or later when he contemplates the "emotion recollected in tranquillity." C. Day Lewis has mentioned that, during World War II, a single line with nostalgic associations kept running through his mind—*the flags, the roundabouts, the gala day*—its music so insistent that it eventually became the germ of a nine-sonnet sequence.

To identify the original stimulus from which a poem grows is often a task for the psychologist rather than the critic or even the poet himself. The most candid author talking voluminously about the development of one of his poems may fail to see or to remember the idea's first glimmerings in his consciousness. Nevertheless, those who hope to write may find it helpful to look at some successful poems to try to reconstruct the ways they might have suggested themselves to the shaping imaginations of their authors. This is a means for discovering where ideas can originate.

One quality that sets the poet apart from most people, a quality he shares with the creative scientist, is an enlarged capacity for observing things around him. His five senses are more often at the ready to experience thoroughly the sights, sounds, tastes, smells, and tactile impressions he encounters. Thousands of pedestrians passing the New York City Public Library have seen a woman feeding the pigeons there. May Swenson, with her poet's keener eye, took in all the details of the woman's dress and posture, the motion of the birds, and the magnificent spectrum of colors displayed in what most observers probably saw as a drab scene. From these observations she made a poem.

Pigeon Woman

Slate, or dirty-marble-colored,
or rusty-iron-colored, the pigeons
on the flagstones in front of the
Public Library make a sharp lake

into which the pigeon woman wades
at exactly 1:30. She wears a
plastic pink raincoat with a round
collar (looking like a little

girl, so gay) and flat gym shoes,
her hair square-cut orange.
Wide-apart feet carefully enter
the spinning, crooning waves

(as if she'd just learned how
to walk, each step conscious,
an accomplishment) blue knots in the
calves of her bare legs (uglied marble),

age in angled cords of jaw
and neck, her pimento-colored hair,
hanging in thin tassels, is gray
around a balding crown.

The day-old bread drops down
from her veined hand dipping out

of a paper sack. Choppy, shadowy ripples,
the pigeons strike around her legs.

Sack empty, she squats and seems to rinse
her hands in them—the rainy greens and
oily purples of their necks. Almost
they let her wet her thirsty fingertips—

but drain away in an untouchable tide.
A make-believe trade
she has come to, in her lostness
or illness or age—to treat the motley

city pigeons at 1:30 every day, in all
weathers. It is for them she colors
her own feathers. Ruddy-footed
on the lime-stained paving,

purling to meet her when she comes,
they are a lake of love. Retreating
from her hands as soon as empty,
they are the flints of love.

—May Swenson (1919–   )

This kind of observation, the impression of a sensory experience on the mind, is the beginning of many poems. Sometimes a poet starts to write in the excitement of the moment while the sight or sound is still tingling his senses. Sometimes he files the observation away in his memory and retrieves it later. Wordsworth, his sister's records say, was delighted with the sight of daffodils that seemed to be dancing at Ullswater; but it was two years later that he made a poem, "I Wandered Lonely as a Cloud," from the experience. Poems often originate in stored memories. A surprise in childhood, a long-dead friend, the chance encounter on a train last year, the way a snow-covered field looked the past spring—these are the kinds of recollections that everyone holds. The poet, though, is more likely to mine this material in his reflections and to sift from it something bright enough to require expression in words.

Sometimes a poem appears to have sprung from the emotions of the poet rather than from what he observes or remembers. He is joyful, or dejected, or angry, or lonely, or loving, or suffused with feelings of religious reverence or patriotism, and words are his way to express and organize these states. Here is an example that remains intense after many centuries:

> Western wind, when will thou blow?
> The small rain down can rain.
> Christ, that my love were in my arms,
> And I in my bed again.
>
> —Anonymous Middle English Lyric

These lines seem to have originated in the poet's feeling— an unusual combination of erotic yearning and homesickness. There is, of course, an implicit interdependence between emotion and observation or memory. A poet's feelings can cast their color on all he sees and remembers. Or something seen or recalled can produce strong feelings.

Some poems grow from what is inventively imagined rather than seen, or remembered, or felt. By rearranging and elaborating impressions from experience, the poet can create something that is quite new. The following poem invents a dramatic scene with speaking characters:

Piazza Piece

> —I am a gentleman in a dustcoat trying
> To make you hear. Your ears are soft and small
> And listen to an old man not at all,
> They want the young men's whispering and sighing.
> But see the roses on your trellis dying

And hear the spectral singing of the moon;
For I must have my lovely lady soon,
I am a gentleman in a dustcoat trying.

—I am a lady young in beauty waiting
Until my true love comes, and then we kiss.
But what gray man among the vines is this
Whose words are dry and faint as in a dream?
Back from my trellis, Sir, before I scream!
I am a lady young in beauty waiting.

                    —John Crowe Ransom (1888–   )

A word of caution may be useful to those with less skill than John Crowe Ransom. To invent a situation or feeling always carries with it the risk that the poem will turn out to appear artificial and unconvincing. That tiresome admonition offered to all beginning writers—"Write about what you *know*" —is sound advice for most novice poets.

Besides observation, memory, feelings, and inventive imagination, there is another kind of stimulation that can compel the writing of a poem. The author may be intrigued with a complicated idea, some event or situation or philosophic concept, to the point where he wants to work out its implications in poetic form. Archibald MacLeish wished to enunciate some precepts about what a poem ought to be, and so wrote these lines:

Ars Poetica

A poem should be palpable and mute
As a globed fruit,

Dumb
As old medallions to the thumb,

Silent as the sleeve-worn stone
Of casement ledges where the moss has grown—

A poem should be wordless
As the flight of birds.

A poem should be motionless in time
As the moon climbs,

Leaving, as the moon releases
Twig by twig the night-entangled trees,

Leaving, as the moon behind the winter leaves,
Memory by memory the mind—

A poem should be motionless in time
As the moon climbs.

A poem should be equal to:
Not true.

For all the history of grief
An empty doorway and a maple leaf.

For love
The leaning grasses and two lights above the sea—

A poem should not mean
But be.

—Archibald MacLeish (1892–   )

If a poem comments on an immediate event or situation that has public as well as personal significance, it is usually called a TOPICAL POEM or OCCASIONAL POEM. These designations would apply, for example, to poems written in response to President Kennedy's assassination or to the lunar landings.

Even with all these sources of ideas for poems, the new writer is often discouraged. "What can I observe or feel or think of," he is likely to ask, "that hasn't already been put into a poem, and by a better writer?" It is true that the likeliest subjects—nature, love, death, fame, piety, work, war, the passage of time, and the transience of human experience—have already inspired hundreds of poems. But there are still opportunities to be fresh and original. The poet can, for example, bring what he sees or remembers into connection with something else, something usually quite separate. "Pigeon Woman" does just this. What the poet saw—an unattractive woman feeding birds—is expressed in a way that suggests another idea—that the birds form a kind of lake around the woman, a lake that recedes when the food is gone. Because of words like *lake, wades, raincoat, waves, dipping, choppy, ripples, rinse, rainy, wet, thirsty, drain, tide,* a landlocked scene seems to become watery. In the end, the scene dries up; the water drains off, and only flints remain. The subjects for poems may indeed be limited, but the possibilities for combining ideas are not likely to be exhausted for as far ahead as the imagination can reach.

JOURNAL PROJECTS

1. List five or six commonplace items in your immediate environment. Make detailed sensory observations of each, writing down as many qualities as you can discover. Be sure to consider touch, taste, and smell as well as the more frequently explored sensations of sight and sound.
2. Keep a careful record over the next month of all the ideas for poems that come to mind. For each, try to identify the source of the idea, whether observation, memory, emotion, inventive imagination, philosophic contemplation, or some combination of these stimuli.
3. Identify the current news item that is most interesting to you. Is it good material for a topical poem? How would you begin to develop the idea poetically?
4. Think about the following topics for poems. For each, suggest some normally unrelated idea that your mind associates with the topic in order to produce an original subject:

a. A fountain.
b. Moon rocks.
c. The discovery of an old photograph of yourself as a child.
d. A feeling of sudden anger.
e. Air pollution.

ESTABLISHING THE INTENTIONS
OF THE POEM

An artist with an idea does not proceed very far in painting his picture without some broad but firm intentions about how the finished composition will look. He decides whether his picture will try to simulate something in the world outside, or whether it will represent that something in a kind of artistic shorthand, or whether it will avoid any attempt to imitate the real world in favor of surrealism or abstract design. He thinks about the viewing distance through which his picture will most effectively make its impression. He knows what kind of impression he hopes his work will make, whether the viewer is to be delighted by beauty, disturbed by violence, intrigued by detail, amused by novelty and humor. These intentions govern his decisions about color, form, and arrangement, and the very brush strokes through which he transforms his idea into an artistic entity.

A poem, too, is an intricate composition, and the work involved in its making deserves careful advance plans, the establishment of its intentions. There are two kinds of decisions a writer ought to make before he begins the actual work of putting a poem together. He should, first of all, know what the process of the poem is to be. Will it narrate an event or a series of events? Will it describe some person, place, object, or feeling? Will it suggest or develop an idea?

A NARRATIVE POEM is one whose meaning is principally tied to events. It relates some movement from *A* to *B,* and the space between those points can be as narrow as the mouse's running up the clock and down again or as wide as the wanderings of Odysseus over ten years. The poem can include one action or several, the events can be trivial or earth-shaking, the material preposterous or realistic, the mood humorous or grave. Epics, popular ballads, and most nursery rhymes are narrative poems, and so are such diverse stories in verse as Keats's "The Eve of St. Agnes," Longfellow's "Paul Revere's Ride," and Robert Frost's "Out, Out—." The term "narrative poem" suggests to many a detailed and complete story, but the classification also includes short segments of stories like this one:

Eight O'Clock

He stood, and heard the steeple
  Sprinkle the quarters on the morning town.
One, two, three, four, to market-place and people
  It tossed them down.

Strapped, noosed, nighing his hour,
  He stood and counted them and cursed his luck;
And then the clock collected in the tower
  Its strength, and struck.

—A. E. Housman (1859–1936)

These lines unfold one ultimate event in what must be a long history—the public execution of an unnamed man for an unspecified crime.

A DESCRIPTIVE POEM may have motion in it, but its principal focus is upon selecting and presenting those details that will convey a scene, a sound, a personality, a feeling in a way that can be clearly grasped by the reader. If "Eight O'Clock" used its eight lines mainly to develop the scene of the hanging in memorable detail or to explore the feelings of the condemned man instead of subordinating them to the event, it would be a descriptive poem. "Pigeon Woman" (p. 4) describes a person in a particular setting, and "Western Wind" (p. 6) describes the feelings of the speaker.

The poem whose business it is to suggest or develop an idea is dominated by the idea that lurks within whatever details the poem includes. "Ars Poetica," for example, contains many small descriptions, but they all contribute to the central theme—a set of rules about poetry. Here is a short poem that was inspired by something the poet saw, but is plainly intent not on describing but on putting forth an idea:

On Seeing Weather-Beaten Trees

Is it as plainly in our living shown,
By slant and twist, which way the wind hath blown?

—Adelaide Crapsey (1878–1914)

A poem can, of course, combine narration, description, and the presentation of an idea, and a work with the scope of *The Divine Comedy* can easily include large measures of all three. Even there, however, one kind of process—the presentation of the idea—is the first intention. In a short poem, it is especially important that the writer emphasize one of these intentions if the finished work is to seem unified.

Before he sets seriously to work, the poet should also ask himself why he is writing the poem. Has he some feeling that he needs to ventilate? Does he wish to amuse himself or his reader? Does he hope to encourage his reader to entertain some thought or to experience some emotion? Or does he intend to change attitudes or rally others to a cause—to war or to work or to merrymaking? These purposes need not be mutually exclusive. A single poem can express the author's feelings, arouse feelings in the reader, and try to put that reader into a frame of mind where he will adopt a particular attitude. However complex the poem's intended function, though, the work will proceed more effectively if the poet thoroughly understands all its complexities.

The anonymous "Western Wind" (p. 6) seems clearly an outcry from the deep feelings of the poet, perhaps an English soldier on the Continent, yearning for the gentler weather and the domestic and amorous security of home. One thinks of this kind of poem as partly therapeutic in its purposes, a way for the poet to "let off steam," to dissipate an inner intensity through words. The following poem may also have originated in an intense feeling. If so, the emotion has been refined, translated into a more restrained statement. The poem's intentions do not seem obviously related to the release of feelings. It is relaxed, unimpassioned, detached, rather elegant:

Nude Descending a Staircase

Toe upon toe, a snowing flesh,
A gold of lemon, root and rind,
She sifts in sunlight down the stairs
With nothing on. Nor on her mind.

We spy beneath the banister
A constant thresh of thigh on thigh—
Her lips imprint the swinging air
That parts to let her parts go by.

One-woman waterfall, she wears
Her slow descent like a long cape
And pausing, on the final stair
Collects her motions into shape.

—X. J. Kennedy (1929–   )

The process of this poem is descriptive, but its function is to amuse; the poet entertains himself by translating a picture into words and entertains his reader with a collage of color and motion.

Some poems indicate their authors' more urgent needs to convey feeling or thought; the poem becomes a method for convincing or teaching the reader. This is evident in "Pigeon Woman" (p. 4). The *lostness, illness, age* that draw the lonely woman towards her birds evoke compassion and pity in the reader and a sense of regret that the birds are so selfish and self-serving in offering only temporary companionship. Conveying thought rather than feeling, "Ars Poetica" (p. 7) presents a lesson about poetry, a way of trying to make the reader understand what a poem ought to be.

The persuasive poem that deliberately and directly sets out to change attitudes or to produce action has taken various modes in different eras. Poetic satire, aimed at social or aesthetic reform, which made up much of Pope's work and the work of his eighteenth-century contemporaries, is rare in the twentieth century. There is some evidence, though, that such poetry may again become popular. A recent resurgence of satire in the drama and the stage revue suggests that poets who seek to encourage changes in their environment through satire may find an audience waiting.

Many conventional classes of persuasive poetry—the drinking song, the thanksgiving hymn, the work song, the call to arms—have traditionally been written to be sung. Anthologies often include examples from the past by authors more firmly remembered for less singable poetry. In this century, strangely, those who write lyrics for songs are usually a group apart from what are called "serious poets." Such separation may be artificial and temporary. Anne Sexton's readings of her poems to the accompaniment of a "rock" group have been enthusiastically received. Some lyrics by the Beatles, Simon and Garfunkel, and Leonard Cohen demonstrate that in popular music the words need not be mere doggerel of the *June/moon/spoon/soon* variety to fill out the rhythm, but can, instead, be as stimulating as the music. Such song lyrics often have an intent that is persuasive in rather an indirect way.

The twentieth-century poet who wishes to influence opinion typically uses stark realism and forceful expressions and associations to shock his reader into recognizing a wrong that needs amendment or a neglected value that needs support. The stresses circumscribing many lives in the years since the outbreak of World War II have impelled poets like Randall Jarrell, Allen Ginsberg, and James Wright towards this kind of poetic persuasion. Here is a poem of Jarrell's about a World War II experience:

Eighth Air Force

If, in an odd angle of the hutment,
A puppy laps the water from a can
Of flowers, and the drunk sergeant shaving
Whistles *O Paradiso!*—shall I say that man
Is not as men have said: a wolf to man?

The other murderers troop in yawning;
Three of them play Pitch, one sleeps, and one
Lies counting missions, lies there sweating
Till even his heart beats: One; One; One.
O murderers! . . . Still, this is how it's done:

This is a war. . . . But since these play, before they die,
Like puppies with their puppy; since, a man,
I did as these have done, but did not die—
I will content the people as I can
And give up these to them: Behold the man!

I have suffered, in a dream, because of him,
Many things; for this last saviour, man,

I have lied as I lie now. But what is lying?
Men wash their hands, in blood, as best they can.
I find no fault in this just man.

                    —Randall Jarrell (1914–1965)

Here a detailed description of soldiers at rest between missions leads to an intense revulsion against war as legal murder, of which the speaker is guilty along with the rest of the soldiers. A participant in this deadly game, he associates himself with Pontius Pilate, too weak to dissent from the general will or habit. The poem does not specifically say, "War is evil," or "Just men will refuse to fight and kill." Yet the reader cannot help but receive messages like these. He is meant to receive them, and to have his attitude, perhaps his efforts, turned towards peace.

These two questions, then, are important for the poet to answer before the hard work of composition gets fully underway. What is the process of my poem to be—narration, description, or the presentation of an idea? Why am I writing this poem? In establishing his intentions in these areas, the author furnishes himself with goals and also with limits against extravagant digression.

JOURNAL PROJECTS

5. Using the same form and introducing whatever new material seems relevant, try to rewrite "Eight O'Clock" as a descriptive poem that focuses on either the scene of the execution or on the feelings of the condemned man.
6. Keep a record for the next month of all your impulses to write a poem. Record each time the reason you want to write the poem, what function you think it will serve. Do you want to release your own feelings? To entertain yourself or your readers? To convey an emotion or an idea? To change attitudes or incite action?

7. Think of a subject on which you have strong convictions about which you would like to persuade others. Could this persuading be effectively accomplished in a poem? How would you begin writing it?

BEGINNING WITH A FORM

The form a poem will take is usually not the poet's first thought. Typically, he begins to put ideas or feelings into words, jotting down images, metaphors, alternate phrases. Somewhere along the way, he probably stops to ask, "What form should the whole poem have?" and begins to consider those possibilities that look most promising.

Some poems, though, begin with a prescribed form. To start this way may seem humdrum and mechanical compared with being inspired by vivid observations or strong emotions. But deliberate formal beginnings have produced some great poetry: Shakespeare's sonnets apparently grew from the intention to write sonnets rather than poems about love, fame, and death; the philosophic arguments and exquisite locutions of Pope's *Moral Essays* were cast to fit the preaccepted mold of the heroic couplet.

There are times when beginning with a form is the best or the only way. When the novice is uncertain about how to get started, when the experienced poet's fountains of inspiration have temporarily trickled dry, when any writer wants the deliberate discipline of working precisely with words, then the choice of a form can be the decision that unblocks the mind and makes work possible. Those who paint or draw or make sculptures often begin with the idea of what they want to develop. But sometimes they begin with a space that has to be filled—the dimensions of the canvas or page, the niche in the wall, the border area to be decorated. Starting with a form is like starting with this kind of shape in which to enclose the poem.

Among all the forms that poetry can take, the one that is often said to be most "natural" for writers in English is BLANK VERSE. Blank verse consists of unrhymed lines. Each line is a PENTAMETER, that is, it includes five metric feet; and each foot is an IAMB. An iamb is a two-syllable unit, the first syllable unstressed, the second syllable stressed. Words like *today, respect,* and *believe* are iambs. When each is pronounced, the emphasis falls on the second syllable. In this connection, it is interesting to look again at the words that nudged C. Day Lewis to write his poems—*the flags, the roundabouts, the gala day.* In reading this aloud, one naturally alternates unstressed and stressed syllables all along the line. There are five such pairs, as the diagram below illustrates; the line is an IAMBIC PENTAMETER line:

$$\text{the flags,} \mid \text{the round} \mid \text{abouts,} \mid \text{the ga} \mid \text{la day.}$$

Once the beat of iambic pentameter is understood, one can speak or jot down all kinds of ideas in this form to make units of blank verse. Since no rhyme is needed and since the rhythm of English speech often alternates unstressed and stressed syllables, practicing blank verse isn't difficult. Here are some nearly spontaneous communications, the kind that can be devised by anyone who keeps the blank-verse rhythm in mind:

> While walking in the garden, I observe
> The rhododendron is in bloom again,
> And all the mountain laurel bushes too.
>
> Hello, Miss Murphy, can you spare the time
> To help me with my homework? I must write

An essay on the cotton gin and its
Effects on agriculture in the south.

Two astronauts have landed on the moon
And spoken to us over miles of space.
The miracle of watching while they walked
Upon that other planet made our world
Seem small, but less alone, less self-contained.

These lack the fresh perceptions and careful word choices of good poetry, but all conform to the definition of blank verse. By choosing and arranging words to fit this rhythm, one can cast many kinds of ideas, simple or complicated, trivial or profound, into blank verse. When a beginning poet has an easy familiarity with this form, he may wish to try a blank-verse poem, that is, a series of lines that not only follow the blank-verse rhythm but also say something significant in the distinctive language of a poetic utterance. Here is a good example:

The Map-Maker on His Art

After the bronzed, heroic traveler
Returns to the television interview
And cocktails at the Ritz, I in my turn
Set forth across the clean, uncharted paper.
Smiling a little at his encounters with
Savages, bugs, and snakes, for the most part
Skipping his night thoughts, philosophic notes,
Rainy reflexions, I translate his trip
Into my native tongue of bearings, shapes,
Directions, distances. My fluent pen
Wanders and cranks as his great river does,
Over the page, making the lonely voyage
Common and human.
              This my modest art
Brings wilderness well down into the range
Of any budget; under the haunted mountain
Where he lay in delirium, deserted

By his safari, they will build hotels
In a year or two. I make no claim that this
Much matters (they will name a hotel for him
And none for me), but lest the comparison
Make me appear a trifle colorless,
I write the running river a rich blue
And—let imagination rage!—wild green
The jungles with their tawny meadows and swamps
Where, till the day I die, I will not go.

                                        —Howard Nemerov (1920–   )

If all these lines were in absolutely regular blank verse, the effect would be monotonous. To avoid this, the author has allowed variations to assert themselves, as they do in language naturally. When the fourth line is marked for syllables and stresses, one notices that there is an extra, unstressed syllable at the end:

Sĕt fórth | ăcróss | thĕ cleán, | ŭnchárt | ĕd páp | ĕr.

That extra syllable is called a FEMININE ENDING because it is "weak" as opposed to a "strong" (stressed) MASCULINE END-ING. There are three other lines in the poem with feminine endings.

Variations within the line are also possible:

Skíppĭng | hĭs níght | thoúghts, phí | lŏsó | phĭc notés

Of these five metric feet, only the second, fourth, and fifth are iambs. The first foot is just the reverse of an iamb, with the stressed syllable first, followed by an unstressed syllable. That foot is called a TROCHEE and can be illustrated by such words as *slowly, muffin, mortar*. (At least ten other lines in the poem begin with trochees.) The third foot in the line contains two equally stressed syllables and is called a SPONDEE. Words like *freight-train, daybreak,* and *shamrock* are all spondees. Other metric feet that can be substituted for the iamb in blank verse are the DACTYL (a stressed syllable followed by two unstressed syllables, as in *suddenly, generous,* and *sheltering*) and the ANAPEST (two unstressed syllables followed by a stressed syllable, as in *interrupt, understand,* and *indirect*). When a poem is said to be in blank verse, what is really meant is that most of the lines have five feet and most of those feet are iambs. But within this dominant pattern, as in almost all patterns. for poetry, there is room for experiment and variety.

Blank verse has played a major part in the progress of English poetry. From Christopher Marlowe's first play (*Tamburlaine-I*) in 1587 until the closing of the theatres in 1642, the period of England's great dramatic Renaissance, blank verse was the principal form for plays, including Shakespeare's. Writers from Milton to Robert Frost have used it as the vehicle for narrative poetry. It is a form that can be usefully considered for a poem likely to extend beyond eight lines where the subject is a serious one and the mood dignified. Emerson's "Days," Tennyson's "Ulysses," and Wallace Stevens's "Sunday Morning" illustrate skillful uses of this form.

A striking difference in the sound and the pace of iambic pentameter lines is introduced when they are rhymed in pairs or COUPLETS. The voice that recites, the eye that reads, the ear that hears them awaits the two-line unit that the rhymed syllables describe:

The Silver Swan

The silver swan, who living had no note,
When death approached, unlocked her silent throat;
Leaning her breast against the reedy shore,
Thus sung her first and last, and sung no more:
Farewell, all joys; O death, come close mine eyes;
More geese than swans now live, more fools than wise.

—Anonymous (c. 1612)

The metrical arrangement of these quaint and old-fashioned lines is the same as in a blank-verse poem. Iambic pentameter is the dominant meter, the iamb replaced occasionally for variation. (*Leaning* in line 3 is a trochee; *More geese* and *more fools* in line 6 would probably be read as spondees.) The rhymes, however, add another kind of design to that provided by meter, binding pairs of lines together, providing satisfaction to the ear or to the mind's ear whenever a line's final word is echoed by its rhyming partner. In "The Silver Swan," each two-line rhyme unit corresponds to a unit of syntax and of the idea that the poem develops. The pairs of lines are, therefore, called CLOSED COUPLETS. A closed-couplet poem can have any even number of lines, from two lines to hundreds. But, however long, each couplet will enclose a substantially complete segment. Here are some extracts from the works of Alexander Pope (1688–1744), who typically wrote long poems in closed couplets:

> 'Tis with our judgments as our watches, none
> Go just alike, yet each believes his own.
>
> —from "Essay on Criticism," Part I

> True ease in writing comes from art, not chance,
> As those move easiest who have learn'd to dance.
> 'Tis not enough no harshness gives offence;
> The sound must seem an echo to the sense.
>
> —from "Essay on Criticism," Part II

> For forms of government let fools contest;
> Whate'er is best administer'd is best;
> For modes of faith let graceless zealots fight;
> His can't be wrong whose life is in the right.
> In faith and hope the world will disagree,
> But all mankind's concern is charity.
>
> —from "Essay on Man," Epistle III

It is easy to see the unit that each pair of lines forms, even when that unit is part of a larger idea. Of the six lines that comprise the last example, the first, third, and fifth set forth ideas of contention; the second, fourth, and sixth, corresponding ideas of settlement and harmony. The six-line statement, then, is composed of three smaller units, each a closed couplet.

All but one of these lines by Pope are END-STOPPED; that is, they culminate in a mark of punctuation that signals some pause in the sense. When a line does not end with such a pause, as in the first of Pope's lines quoted, it is called a RUN-ON LINE. The experienced reader will move on without pause for breath. The run-on quality of a line is more technically referred to as ENJAMBMENT. When there is enjambment between one rhyming pair and the next, the lines are called OPEN COUPLETS. The beginning of Robert Browning's "My Last Duchess" illustrates the looser, more flowing effect that the open couplet makes possible:

> That's my last Duchess painted on the wall,
> ** Looking as if she were alive. I call
> * That piece a wonder, now: Frà Pandolf's hands
> Worked busily a day, and there she stands.
> * Will't please you sit and look at her? I said
> ** "Frà Pandolf" by design, for never read
> Strangers like you that pictured countenance,
> The depth and passion of its earnest glance,
> * But to myself they turned (since none puts by
> The curtain I have drawn for you, but I)
> And seemed as they would ask me, if they durst,
> ** How such a glance came there; so, not the first
> Are you to turn and ask thus. . . .

Those lines marked with asterisks illustrate enjambment. Where there is a double asterisk, the line runs on into the next couplet. A pause within a line, like the pause after *alive* in the second line of Browning's poem, is called a CAESURA.

Iambic pentameter couplets, as all these examples have been, are also called HEROIC COUPLETS. The term "couplet," though, refers to the pair of rhymes and not to the meter; so couplets can be made from lines of any meter or length or, indeed, of mixed lengths, as in "Ars Poetica" (p. 7). Writers in English, though, have generally preferred either the pentameter or the tetrameter couplet. A TETRAMETER line consists of four metric feet instead of five. The following poem includes seven closed tetrameter couplets:

Delight in Disorder

A sweet disorder in the dress
Kindles in clothes a wantonness.
A lawn about the shoulders thrown
Into a fine distraction;
An erring lace, which here and there
Enthralls the crimson stomacher,
A cuff neglectful, and thereby
Ribbons to flow confusedly;
A winning wave, deserving note,
In the tempestuous petticoat;
A careless shoestring, in whose tie
I see a wild civility;
Do more bewitch me than when art
Is too precise in every part.

—Robert Herrick (1591–1674)

Couplets are useful to a poet for organizing many different kinds of material, from the two-line aphorism (*Early to bed, early to rise/Makes a man healthy, wealthy, and wise*) to a long narrative like Chaucer's *Canterbury Tales,* from lyrics like "Delight in Disorder" to Pope's extended philosophical and critical treatises. Although the rhyming makes couplets more difficult to write than blank verse, they are, in one sense, more versatile. Like blank verse, they are appropriate for serious subjects and a grave mood. But the pattern imposed by rhyme makes the couplet an apt vehicle for wit, a possibility exploited by Pope in *The Rape of the Lock* and more recently by Robert Frost in "Departmental."

The couplet is the shortest unit in poetry that can constitute a STANZA, that is, a group of lines set off together as a poetic paragraph. In practice, though, the couplet is more often used as a RUNNING FORM, like blank verse, than as a stanzaic unit. Some poets have written in the TRIPLET (also called the TER-CET) stanza, a three-line unit where two or three of the lines rhyme. But the most popular stanza in English has been the QUATRAIN, containing four lines and usually incorporating some rhyme. Quatrains can have various rhythms and sound patterns, since any line length, any metric foot, or any rhyme scheme can be used. Some sample of this diversity is provided in the following poems, all of which use the quatrain stanza:

> Western wind, when will thou blow?
> The small rain down can rain.
> Christ, that my love were in my arms,
> And I in my bed again.

(Alternating iambic tetrameter and iambic TRIMETER [three-foot] lines, with a rhyme scheme *abcb,* often called the BALLAD STANZA because it was a familiar form in popular ballads.)

> Twinkle, twinkle, little star,
> How I wonder what you are!
> Up above the world so high,
> Like a diamond in the sky.
>
> —Popular nursery rhyme

(Trochaic tetrameter lines in which the last foot lacks the un-stressed second syllable, rhyming *aabb.*)

A slumber did my spirit seal;
   I had no human fears:
She seemed a thing that could not feel
   The touch of earthly years.

No motion has she now, no force;
   She neither hears nor sees;
Rolled round in earth's diurnal course,
   With rocks, and stones, and trees.

          —William Wordsworth (1770–1850)

(Alternating iambic tetrameter and iambic trimeter lines; like the ballad stanza, except for the addition of a second pair of rhymes, producing the pattern *abab*.)

On His Seventy-fifth Birthday

I strove with none, for none was worth my strife,
   Nature I loved, and next to Nature, Art;
I warmed both hands before the fire of life,
   It sinks, and I am ready to depart.

          —Walter Savage Landor (1775–1864)

(Four iambic pentameter lines, rhyming *abab;* sometimes called the HEROIC QUATRAIN or the ELEGIAC QUATRAIN.)

The Soul selects her own Society—
Then—shuts the Door—
To her divine Majority—
Present no more—

Unmoved—she notes the Chariots—pausing—
At her low Gate—
Unmoved—an Emperor be kneeling
Upon her Mat—

I've known her—from an ample nation—
Choose One—

Then—close the Valves of her attention—
Like Stone—

—Emily Dickinson (1830–1886)

(Lines of varying length with the iamb as the dominant foot, using a rhyme scheme *abab*.)

As these examples demonstrate, a quatrain can have a sing-song or a dignified pace, absolute regularity or a "sweet disorder," a light-hearted or a ponderous quality, depending on the poet's selections of rhythm and sound. A closer look at the Emily Dickinson poem may encourage a quatrain writer who finds himself frustrated by a paucity of rhyming words in English. It is not always possible to discover EXACT RHYMES like *door/more,* where both the final stressed vowel and the final consonant sounds are identical. For this reason, poets, especially contemporary poets, often resort to IMPERFECT RHYMES. Sometimes they match only the final consonant sound, as in *gate/mat;* sometimes, only the stressed vowel sound, as in *low/moan* or *bread/debt.* There is some confusion about what to call such rhymes; the terms SLANT RHYME, OFF RHYME, NEAR RHYME, HALF RHYME and APPROXIMATE RHYME are used by various critics to describe either or both of these imperfect-rhyme possibilities. Perhaps it is a mistake to use the word "imperfect" at all, since it so strongly suggests a defect. Actually, approximate rhymes can be entirely pleasing; in substituting for the identical rhyming sound something that is close but not identical, they often present the ear with delightful surprises.

A beginning poet who has set himself the task of composing several heroic couplets and heroic quatrains may wish next to attempt an English sonnet. The SONNET has long been the most popular fixed form for English poetry. Whereas poems written in blank verse, couplets, or quatrains can vary in length, the sonnet is typically fourteen lines of iambic pentameter verse incorporating a rhyme pattern. The ENGLISH SONNET, modified from an Italian form in the sixteenth century and most notably utilized by Shakespeare, consists, formally, of three quatrains and a couplet. This technical description, of course, only partly describes what an English sonnet really is. The four component parts should, in a thoroughly successful sonnet, correspond to divisions and interrelationships in the idea of the poem.

Sonnet 73

That time of year thou mayst in me behold
When yellow leaves, or none, or few, do hang
Upon those boughs which shake against the cold,
Bare ruined choirs, where late the sweet birds sang;
In me thou see'st the twilight of such day
As after sunset fadeth in the west,
Which by and by black night doth take away,
Death's second self, that seals up all in rest.
In me thou see'st the glowing of such fire
That on the ashes of his youth doth lie,
As the deathbed whereon it must expire,
Consumed with that which it was nourished by.
This thou perceiv'st, which makes thy love more strong,
To love that well which thou must leave ere long.

—William Shakespeare (1556–1616)

In this famous example, each of the three quatrains consists of a separate statement in which a speaker describes his advancing age in a distinctive way: in the first quatrain, his life is like the autumn of the year; in the second, like the twilight of the day; in the third, like a fire reduced to its embers. The quatrains are thus not only structural but functional divisions of the poem, three descriptions preceding the couplet that expresses appreciation for a lover's constancy despite the encroachments of time. What is more, the three quatrains are not really interchangeable; they cannot be put into a different sequence without loss to the poem. As Shakespeare arranged them, they move from larger to smaller units of time, from daylight to dark, from outdoors to indoors, from numbness to sleep to death. The form has truly been used to maximum advantage in organizing the material of the poem.

The three-quatrain-plus-couplet arrangement that characterizes the English sonnet allows for various kinds of progress within the poem. Three specific examples can be summarized in a generalizing couplet. Or three stages of a short narrative can lead to a couplet that contains the climactic event. Or three propositions can be advanced only to be negated by the counter-argument of the final couplet. Or the couplet can provide the result for three conditions set forth in the quatrains.

One can appreciate the subtle relationship between form and material by comparing the English sonnet with its progenitor. The ITALIAN SONNET is the same in length and meter, but its different rhyme scheme brings about a division within the poem that changes the essential structure. The Italian sonnet has two sections instead of four, an eight-line OCTAVE followed by a six-line SESTET. Within each of these sections there are, if the form is strictly used, only two rhyming sounds. The octave rhyme scheme is *abbaabba;* the sestet can have any of several arrangements for its two sounds (*cdcdcd, cdccdc, cddcdc*), but it typically does not end with a couplet.

On First Looking into Chapman's Homer

Much have I traveled in the realms of gold,
    And many goodly states and kingdoms seen;
    Round many western islands have I been
Which bards in fealty to Apollo hold.

Oft of one wide expanse had I been told
   That deep-browed Homer ruled as his demesne,
   Yet did I never breathe its pure serene
Till I heard Chapman speak out loud and bold:
Then felt I like some watcher of the skies
   When a new planet swims into his ken;
Or like stout Cortez when with eagle eyes
   He stared at the Pacific—and all his men
Looked at each other with a wild surmise—
   Silent, upon a peak in Darien.

—John Keats (1795–1821)

It is easy to discern the two sections of this poem. In the first "movement," Keats gives some general information about his reading, ending with the comment that he never read Homer with delight until he encountered the translation by George Chapman. The second "movement" uses two comparisons to explain the wonder of discovering this version of Homer. The poem divides clearly between the eighth and ninth lines, and some writers who work with the Italian sonnet leave a line blank to mark the place where the poem takes a new turn.

Whether set as one stanza or two, this form of sonnet fits a development that includes one major division. Concrete details elaborated in the first eight lines can lead to a generalization in the last six. Conversely, a general development may begin the poem, illustrated by a specific example in the sestet. The sestet can be used to answer questions raised in the octave, or it can raise questions about statements developed in the octave. The octave may deal with events of the past, the sestet with the present. A dramatic dialogue can be divided between two speakers; "Piazza Piece" (p. 6) is such a sonnet. Even the mood can change between the octave and the sestet.

Writing a sonnet is a demanding discipline that may discourage the novice, but the satisfactions of completing the task are great. There is comfort, too, in realizing that others, even skilled poets, have had trouble adhering strictly to either the Italian or the English form. There are Italian sonnets where the developmental "break" falls somewhere other than at the end of the eighth line, where the sestet includes three rhymes (*cdecde, cdeced,* etc.), where a couplet is used to close the poem. There are "mixed breeds" that begin as English and end as Italian. There are sonnets whose structural segments are not reflected in the way the idea is organized. Gerard Manley Hopkins devised a short or CURTAL SONNET with a six-line "octave" and a four-and-a-half-line "sestet." No academy protects the purity of the sonnet form. Experiments can hope to find favor if they are purposeful.

JOURNAL PROJECTS

8. Observe carefully the room or other setting in which you are now, taking detailed notes. Now try to organize these descriptive notes within twelve lines of blank verse.

9. By changing vocabulary and rearranging words and ideas, turn those twelve lines into six iambic pentameter couplets, of which at least two are open couplets.

10. List all the perfect rhymes you can think of for *leave* (e.g. *weave*). Now list all slant rhymes you can think of in which the vowel sound is like that in *leave* but the final consonant sound is different (e.g. *deed*). Next list all slant rhymes in which the final consonant sound is like that in *leave* but the vowel sound is different (e.g. *of*). Follow the same procedure with one or two other words.

11. Using either exact or slant rhymes and any subject material, write three quatrains, one in ballad stanza like "Western Wind," one like "Twinkle, Twinkle Little Star," and one like "On His Seventy-fifth Birthday."

12. Referring to Shakespeare's "Sonnet 73" as a model, try to construct an English sonnet, taking for your topic three examples,

to be developed in the three quatrains, which lead to a summarizing couplet. Do not be discouraged if some lines seem to resist efforts to improve them or if you cannot complete the project. Date all drafts and keep all drafts.

Лʹ *CHOOSING A FORM TO FIT AN IDEA*

Once a writer has what seems to be a viable idea for a poem and has begun to think about words and phrases, he will be faced with his first large aesthetic decision—the choice of a suitable form. Sometimes the material for a poem seems to dictate its own shape immediately and firmly. More often, the poet must experiment with various alternatives, trying to make the best selection among them. This is so major and so critical a choice that he may change his mind several times in the course of composition.

During the decision process, he will probably consider the qualities of the poem's subject. The size and complexity of his idea and the degree of detail the poem is to encompass will help to determine its length. One would probably not attempt to write about the fall of Rome in one quatrain or the fall of a sparrow in a sequence of sonnets, though both could be reasonable attempts in special circumstances. The way the subject is to be organized may affect a decision about whether or not to divide the poem into stanzas; steps of a poem's development can be emphasized by stanzaic units, a flow or continuum by a running form. The nature of some subjects is enhanced by a definite and obvious pattern involving rhythm or sound repetitions. Some other subjects seem to require an apparently unstructured or "free" form. The degree of seriousness of the sub-

ject and the writer's emotional involvement are further considerations. One would probably not cast an elegy into the jingle
pattern of "Twinkle, Twinkle, Little Star," a series of riddles
into blank verse, or a passionate declaration of love into heroic
couplets. Whatever it is, the form ought to be chosen and affirmed for its positive contribution to the poem, and ought not
to be merely an accident, a careless compromise, or a course of
least resistance. The form of the poem determines in a major
way the poem's effect on the reader, and it should be selected or
devised with both the subject and that effect in view.

How important the choice of form is can be illustrated by
close attention to poems by three different poets. All three
poems look as though they may have had the same kind of
origin, the poet's observation of a specific, small natural event
involving a spider. Speaking generally, one might say that a
spider is the topic of all three poems.

Upon a Spider Catching a Fly

Thou sorrow, venom Elfe:
   Is this thy play,
To spin a web out of thyselfe
   To Catch a Fly?
    For Why?

I saw a pettish wasp
   Fall foule therein.
Whom yet thy whorle pins did not clasp
   Lest he should fling
    His sting.

But as affraid, remote
   Didst stand hereat
And with thy little fingers stroke
   And gently tap
    His back.

Thus gently him didst treate
  Lest he should pet,
And in a froppish, waspish heate
  Should gently fret
    Thy net.

Whereas the silly Fly,
  Caught by its leg
Thou by the throate tookst hastily,
  And 'hinde the head
    Bite Dead.

This goes to pot, that not
  Nature doth call.
Strive not above what strength hath got
  Lest in the brawle
    Thou fall.

This Frey seems thus to us.
  Hells Spider gets
His intrails spun to whip Cords thus
  And wove to nets
    And sets.

To tangle Adams race
  In's stratigems
To their Destructions, spoil'd, made base
  By venom things
    Damn'd Sins.

But mighty, Gracious Lord
  Communicate
Thy Grace to breake the Cord, afford
  Us Glorys Gate
    And State

We'l Nightingaile sing like
  When pearcht on high
In Glories Cage, thy glory, bright

Yea, thankfully,
        For joy.

                          —Edward Taylor (1645?–1729)

What Taylor appears to have observed was a spider in its web, carefully placating a wasp that could be dangerous to him but ruthlessly killing a weaker fly. This homely occurrence associated itself in Taylor's mind, possibly because he was a clergyman, with the idea of man's being caught in the devil's web, either as a strong wasp, capable of escaping evil for salvation, or as a silly fly, hopelessly damned. The lines that begin with an address to the spider move on to a teaching sermon and end with a prayer to God for strength and help. The real subject of the poem is not simply a spider preying on insects but the analogy between the spider motif and man's precarious state.

The transition from natural event to religious speculation, from a playful, scolding address to the spider to a reverent appeal to God, must have posed a problem for Edward Taylor in choosing his form. His typical preferences, the heroic couplet or the six-line, rhymed iambic-pentameter stanza, apparently did not satisfy his sense of what this poem should be, possibly because those forms have more measured dignity than the playful talking to a spider might warrant. Yet a pattern so informal as to shut out serious material would have been unsuitable for the second half of the poem. To meet a double need, Taylor constructed a five-line stanza adaptable to the two kinds of material and the two tones that the poem encompasses. Using the iamb as the basic foot, each stanza follows a rigid pattern: there are three feet in the first line, two in the second, four in the third, two in the fourth, one in the fifth. Each stanza has the same rhyme scheme, *ababb*, although the rhymes are often slant rhymes. The change in tone that the progress of the subject requires is effected by a change in the kind of vocabu-

lary. *Is this thy play* (stanza 1) may be metrically like its coun-
terpart, *Communicate* (stanza 9), but the effect of the first is
familiar and casual; of the second, learned and deliberate. A
similar contrast is evident between *And with thy little fingers
stroke* (stanza 3) and *Strive not above what strength hath got*
(stanza 6). The form, though regular, is magnificently adaptable, an admirable solution to the special problems inherent in
the subject.

Although this second poem proceeds from the same kind of
observation, how different its real subject is, and how different
the form to express that subject appropriately:

A Noiseless Patient Spider

A noiseless patient spider,
I mark'd where on a little promontory it stood isolated,
Mark'd how to explore the vacant vast surrounding,
It launch'd forth filament, filament, filament, out of itself,
Ever unreeling them, ever tirelessly speeding them.

And you O my soul where you stand,
Surrounded, detached, in measureless oceans of space,
Ceaselessly musing, venturing, throwing, seeking the spheres to
    connect them,
Till the bridge you will need be form'd, till the ductile anchor hold,
Till the gossamer thread you fling catch somewhere, O my soul.

                    —Walt Whitman (1819–1892)

Whitman's interest in the spider was in its repeated efforts
to begin building a web. The purpose of the web for trapping,
the idea of the spider as predator, the fate of the victims, the
symmetrical beauty of the finished web are of no concern in
this poem. Whitman's response to the spider is more like Robert Bruce's than Edward Taylor's. Yet, like Taylor's, Whitman's subject is complex—the analogy between a spider trying
to attach its filament and his own "soul" trying to find a con-

nection with something firm outside itself. These two very different elements need to be linked, and the form of the poem is one method of linking them.

Whitman chose FREE VERSE as his vehicle. There are two stanzas for developing the two halves of the comparison, and the first line of each is comparatively short; otherwise, there is little semblance of a fixed pattern. The lines vary in length and meter. There is no rhyme scheme. How suitable is this relatively free organization for the poem's subject and for the impression the poem is meant to convey to the reader? Whitman's poem deals with two processes, neither of which reaches any culmination in the poem. Will the spider succeed? Will the soul succeed in its comparable effort? The lines state only that the effort goes on despite initial failures. For such unfinished business, a poetic form that does not reach any prescribed "finish" seems appropriate. The climactic conclusion of a sonnet, or the completed rhymes of couplets, even the measured regularity of blank verse would convey more order and certainty than the quests of the poem imply. Something looser, more varied, less dominated by design is a better choice. The looseness increases as the poem develops; whereas the first stanza is one long sentence, the whole second stanza is a sentence fragment, syntactically incomplete.

Within his two stanzas, Whitman has emphasized the idea of repeated trial and error by repeating words and sounds. The three appearances of *filament* in sequence, the piling up of participles in lines 5 and 8, the recurrence of *till* in lines 9 and 10, the "o" sounds in *O, soul, oceans, throwing,* and *hold* all contribute to the sense of continuing search. This is free verse only insofar as "free" means not rigidly and predictably patterned. The shape of the poem, its rhythm, its syntax, its word choices are fitted to the subject and to the desired impression for the whole poem.

Moving ahead one century, one encounters a third, and again a very different, look at a spider:

Design

I found a dimpled spider, fat and white,
On a white heal-all, holding up a moth
Like a white piece of rigid satin cloth—
Assorted characters of death and blight
Mixed ready to begin the morning right,
Like the ingredients of a witches' broth—
A snow-drop spider, a flower like froth,
And dead wings carried like a paper kite.

What had that flower to do with being white,
The wayside blue and innocent heal-all?
What brought the kindred spider to that height,
Then steered the white moth thither in the night?
What but design of darkness to appall?—
If design govern in a thing so small.

—Robert Frost (1874–1963)

There is much less motion in what Frost observed than in the scenes observed by the other two poets. He saw a frozen tableau, drained of color—a white spider on a white flower, holding up a white moth that it had killed. The observation led him not to speculations on sin and redemption nor to concerns about some comparable psychological state, but to abstract questions about the meaning of this small detail in the natural landscape. How could three things of freak whiteness be brought together in this convergence of albinos? Could it have been by some designing power? Is the power good, evil, or of neutral value like the scientist's natural forces? If this rather cruel event was programmed by some design, what are the implications of such control for the rest of the natural world? These questions are not answered in the poem, which ends with an "if" clause. The reader is left with his own open-ended, somewhat chilling speculations.

But the clear possibility of a design that is purposeful as well as visual, affirmed in the title, is emphasized in the form of the poem. This is not only a sonnet, but a kind of Italian super-sonnet with an extra share of rhyme; one of the octave rhymes is carried into the sestet. Although its implications are vague, the scene that Frost observed was organized into a pattern of visual unity. And, as a parallel, although the questions of the poem remain unsettled, they are presented in a pattern that is unusually tight and controlled.

Pope's dictum—*The sound must seem an echo to the sense* —is heeded in all three of these poems. Frost's uses a fixed form made even more rigid than its conventions require. Taylor's uses an invented regular form. Whitman's uses free verse. Each choice seems right for its own special view of the spider, and each conveys a distinct impression to the reader.

JOURNAL PROJECTS

13. Think about the following subjects for poems and jot down the form(s) you consider to be the most promising for the development of each:

   a. A comparison of the lunar landing with Columbus's first voyage.
   b. The fantasy of discovering buried treasure.
   c. The feeling of being lost.
   d. The death of Cleopatra.
   e. The death of someone you know.

14. Return to the couplets you wrote for Project #9. Turn these six couplets into three quatrains. What difference does this change in form make in your idea and in the total effect of the poem?

ぴ WRITING FREE VERSE

The search for a suitable form should be part of the process of making a poem for any poet who begins with an idea. Keeping in mind his subject, his feelings about it, and the impression he wants his poem to make upon readers, he must consider those forms that look promising and ultimately select from among them. Free verse—verse that is not committed to a predictable pattern of rhythm, rhyme, or stanza—is one of his options.

Some poets, especially if they are young and new to the work of poetry, regard patterns that are not "free" as obstacles to be avoided. They often buttress their avoidance by insisting that regularities in poetry are old-fashioned or unnatural or stifling to the creative impulse. All of these arguments are partly valid. Apparent freedom from pattern is more frequently encountered in poetry of the past hundred years than in earlier poetry. But such freedom, used with purposeful sensitivity by a procession of fine poets—Walt Whitman, Ezra Pound, William Carlos Williams, and others— is an additional possibility in the range of forms, not a superseding substitute. Many contemporary poets still rely heavily on formal patterns, some traditional, some new and inventive.

The words "natural" and "unnatural" as related to poetry are slippery descriptions because the criterion on which they

43

pivot is hard to fix. If "natural" refers to the way people talk or write spontaneously, then most poetic lines, stanzas, rhymes, and rhythms must be relegated to the realm of the unnatural. But any poem, whether formal or "free," is a made thing (indeed, a prose sentence is usually a made thing), and it may be self-defeating to insist that it appear utterly spontaneous. The poet, like the painter, is supposed to select and shape the myriad random data of experience, and his organization involves not only subjects but forms. A creative impulse may not include the predilection for pattern; but a good poem builds from the impulse to a finished structure, and such building involves the poet in a decision about form.

Much of the preference for free verse arises from a delusion that, having no "requirements" for rhythm and rhyme schemes, line lengths, stanzaic shapes, etc., it is easy to write. One would not expect good poetry to emerge from such negative reasons for choosing a form and, as John Ciardi has observed, "Free verse is only easy to write badly." The "free" in "free verse" may suggest a liberation from conventional forms; it does not imply anarchy except to those who have inadequate experience in reading competent free verse and therefore lack the background for trying to write it competently.

Free verse that is effective is distinguished not by what it lacks but by what it owns. A regular rhyme scheme may be missing, but it can be replaced by recurrences of like or similar sounds in a sequence that, if unpredictable, is nonetheless pleasing to the ear. Metrical precision may be missing, but it can be replaced by cadence that has its own pace and rhythm; indeed, Amy Lowell, an eminent proponent of free verse, suggested that "cadenced verse" would be a more accurate label. Free verse may have no stanzaic pattern, but this is often replaced by repeated words, phrases, and lines that give shape to the poem by suggesting a refrain. A poet should choose free verse as he would choose any other form—

because it is the best form for his poem. And he should use its flexibility not as an avoidance tactic but as a positive response to the needs of what he wants to say.

Free verse may be a favorite choice of many modern poets, but it is not really new. Many parts of the Bible have the sound and cadence of free verse, especially the *Psalms*. Here is "Psalm 70" in the King James version:

Make haste, O God, to deliver me; make haste to help me, O Lord.
Let them be ashamed and confounded that seek after my soul; let them be turned backward, and put to confusion, that desire my hurt.
Let them be turned back for a reward of their shame that say, Aha, aha.
Let all those that seek thee rejoice and be glad in thee: and let such as love thy salvation say continually, Let God be magnified.
But I am poor and needy; make haste unto me, O God: thou art my help and my deliverer; O Lord, make no tarrying.

These lines are not metrical, but they are certainly rhythmic. The repeated expressions, *make haste, O God, O Lord, let them, let,* give the psalm resonance, shape, and unity. The reader is conscious of a human voice speaking in incantation, a sound quality that can be attained in free verse more readily than in regular forms.

The simulation of voice cadences is, indeed, one of the conspicuous benefits of good free verse. One can "hear," for example, these two different voices speaking in Walt Whitman's "Out of the Cradle Endlessly Rocking":

Out of the cradle endlessly rocking,
Out of the mocking-bird's throat, the musical shuttle,
Out of the Ninth-month midnight,
Over the sterile sands and the fields beyond, where the child leaving
    his bed wander'd alone, bareheaded, barefoot,
Down from the shower'd halo,

Up from the mystic play of shadows twining and twisting as if they
    were alive,
Out from the patches of briers and blackberries,
From the memories of the bird that chanted to me,
From your memories sad brother, from the fitful risings and fallings
    I heard,
From under that yellow half-moon late-risen and swollen as if with
    tears,
From those beginning notes of yearning and love there in the mist,
From the thousand responses of my heart never to cease,
From the myriad thence-arous'd words,
From the word stronger and more delicious than any,
From such as now they start the scene revisiting,
As a flock, twittering, rising, or overhead passing,
Borne hither, ere all eludes me, hurriedly,
A man, yet by these tears a little boy again,
Throwing myself on the sand, confronting the waves,
I, chanter of pains and joys, uniter of here and hereafter,
Taking all hints to use them, but swiftly leaping beyond them,
A reminiscence sing.

    This is the voice of the author-speaker, letting his memories
of place and self rush out in words as though he were speaking
aloud. And here is the answering voice of the bird, also in free
verse, but with its own special cadence, breath, music, sound
pattern:

    Hither my love!
    Here I am! here!
    With this just-sustain'd note I announce myself to you,
    This gentle call is for you my love, for you.

    Do not be decoy'd elsewhere,
    That is the whistle of the wind, it is not my voice,
    That is the fluttering, the fluttering of the spray,
    Those are the shadows of leaves.

Such use of free verse to simulate voice cadences has been carried forward by some contemporary poets, certainly by Allen Ginsberg (see, for example, his "Kaddish").

"When," the beginning poet is likely to ask, "is it right to choose free verse?" The pat answer too often comes, "When the feeling is so intense that a formal pattern would seem stifling and unnatural." This is probably very bad advice in most cases. The poet who is writing about a subject in which his emotional involvement is great is likely to spill out too many words in an unorganized torrent. Later he may find it easy to rationalize his excesses as expressions of his deep feeling. Many of the most moving poems about love and death and religious devotion are formal poems. The shaping effect of form and the carefully considered choices of words that form requires often confer forcefulness and impact upon the feeling that would be diffused in free verse.

It is safer to select free verse for reasons other than the poet's emotional intensity. When the action of the poem is chaotic, irregular, unresolved in a firm conclusion, then the cadences of free verse may fortify the sense of that action. Whitman, for example, used free verse to emphasize incompletion in "A Noiseless Patient Spider" (p. 39). Free verse is most useful, though, for its adaptability to the sound of a particular voice or to the silently verbalized thoughts of a particular mind in its musings and free associations.

Good free verse is never totally free. It has something that creates order—rhyme (exact or approximate), cadence, repetition, a consonance with the matter of the poem, a unity of voice. The poet who wants to work with free verse will find it helpful to read T. S. Eliot's dramatic monologue, "The Love Song of J. Alfred Prufrock." This long poem consists of irregular stanzas and lines, and there is no dominant meter. But there are many rhymes, some of them surprising in their

originality like *go/Michelangelo, fingers/malingers, ices/crisis.*
Words and phrases are repeated to give the poem sonority and
pattern. And one is conscious throughout of the voice of the
protagonist, moving through changes in mood, rhythm, and
vocabulary, but always distinctively his own.

JOURNAL PROJECTS

15. Return to the couplets you wrote for Project #9 and then
    turned into quatrains for Project #14. Now put this material
    into a free-verse poem of any length. You have now used the
    same material four times—in blank verse (Project #8), in cou-
    plets, in quatrains, and in free verse. With which form are you
    most satisfied?
16. Return to Project #7, the subject about which you would like
    to persuade a reader. Try to begin a poem on this subject, using
    free verse.

WORKING WITH REPEATING
PATTERNS

Three of the forms already discussed—couplets, quatrains, and sonnets—typically involve repetitions of sound called rhyme, and in most examples of these forms rhyme plays a major role in making the pattern. Those for whom the search for rhymes is difficult may find it refreshing to work with forms where part or all of the sound pattern is achieved from the repetition of words, phrases, or whole lines of poetry.

Popular nursery rhymes often rely on such repetition for their pattern.

> London bridge is falling down,
> Falling down, falling down,
> London bridge is falling down,
> My fair lady.
>
> Take some stones and build it up,
> Build it up, build it up,
> Take some stones and build it up,
> My fair lady.

The inventor of these lines had no rhyming whatever to do, yet he created a rhythmic and satisfying sound pattern. Children's play generates much poetry that involves repetition, like this counting jingle, an accompaniment for bouncing a ball:

> One, two, three, O'Leary,
> Four, five, six, O'Leary,
> Seven, eight, nine, O'Leary,
> Ten, O'Leary,
> Postman.

Repetition is by no means confined to folk poetry. Robert Burns used a line or two of refrain for many of his poems that he intended to be sung, like "Comin' Through the Rye." Even when the words outlast their music, repetition can be valuable in a poem. Here is the second stanza of a social protest song by Burns, hardly ever sung now but often read:

> What though on hamely fare we dine,
>   Wear hodden-gray, and a' that;
> Gie fools their silks, and knaves their wine,
>   A man's a man for a' that:
>   For a' that, and a' that,
>   Their tinsel show, and a' that;
>   The honest man, though e'er sae poor,
>   Is king o' men for a' that.

In each of the poem's five stanzas, Burns has relied on the same pattern of repetition, using *a' that* in the second, fourth, fifth, sixth, and eighth lines.

Repetitions, including refrains, can be used either alone or in combination with rhymes in poems that are not intended for singing. Edgar Allan Poe's "The Raven" has a complicated pattern of meter and rhyme and, in addition, the sonorous repetition of *Nevermore* at the end of each stanza. John Crowe Ransom's "Piazza Piece" (p. 6), substitutes, at the end of both the octave and the sestet, a repeated line for the rhyming line that would normally appear in an Italian sonnet.

Some old French and Italian forms that achieve part of their pattern from the repetition of words or whole lines of poetry have attracted the attention of writers in English within the past century. Among such forms, the shortest and simplest is the TRIOLET, an eight-line poem whose first, fourth, and seventh lines are identical and whose second and eighth lines are also identical. This means that, once the first two lines are established, more than half the poem's length is completed. Not, however, half the poem's demands! The third and fifth lines must rhyme with the first; the sixth, with the second:

A Kiss

Rose kissed me today.
　Will she kiss me tomorrow?
Let it be as it may,
Rose kissed me today.
But the pleasure gives way
　To a savor of sorrow;—
Rose kissed me today—
　Will she kiss me tomorrow?

—Henry Austin Dobson (1840–1921)

Triolets are most successful in trimeter or tetrameter lines. The longer pentameter line is too heavy for this short form. The brevity of the triolet with its echo of the opening lines in the conclusion seems to touch any subject with a gentle levity. The meaning of the words in "A Kiss" includes worry and a measure of sadness. Yet, when those words are arranged in a triolet, the mood becomes less serious, mildly mocking, almost light-hearted.

A repeating pattern with greater length, depth, and density is the VILLANELLE, consisting of five triplets and a quatrain in a pattern involving the repetition of two whole lines and allowing only two rhyming sounds.

Do Not Go Gentle Into That Good Night

X *a* Do not go gentle into that good night,
   b Old age should burn and rave at close of day;
Y *a* Rage, rage against the dying of the light.

   a Though wise men at their end know dark is right,
   b Because their words had forked no lightning they
X *a* Do not go gentle into that good night.

   a Good men, the last wave by, crying how bright
   b Their frail deeds might have danced in a green bay,
Y *a* Rage, rage against the dying of the light.

   a Wild men who caught and sang the sun in flight,
   b And learn, too late, they grieved it on its way,
X *a* Do not go gentle into that good night.

   a Grave men, near death, who see with blinding sight
   b Blind eyes could blaze like meteors and be gay,
Y *a* Rage, rage against the dying of the light.

   a And you, my father, there on the sad height,
   b Curse, bless me now with your fierce tears, I pray.
X *a* Do not go gentle into that good night.
Y *a* Rage, rage against the dying of the light.

—Dylan Thomas (1914–1953)

The *ab* designations indicate the rhyme pattern; the *XY* designations, the repeated lines. It is evident that the repetition of the first and third lines later in the poem lends great weight to these two lines in the villanelle. The poet's problem is to make such repetitions usefully incremental rather than monotonous. Dylan Thomas has managed this by adapting the two key lines to imperative commands in their first and last appearances but to descriptive statements in the enclosed stanzas. The words are the same in all instances, but the meaning changes. Unlike the triolet, the villanelle is best suited to seriousness of both subject and tone. This is not only so when the lines are of pentameter length. Edwin Arlington Robinson's villanelle called "The House on the Hill" demonstrates that even with shorter lines the form seems suited to a reflective, grave, somewhat sad poem.

Perhaps the fixed form that sets the new or practised poet his most rigorous exercise is the SESTINA. Rarely does the material of poetic inspiration demand to be written in this form. The sestina must be deliberately chosen, with full knowledge of its difficulties. Robert Francis has commented, ". . . in starting to write a sestina I was really going against my deepest poetic convictions. For a sestina is an extreme example of a poem written from the outside in, and my way is to write from the inside out." Here is the result of his departure from usual practice, his starting with the frame rather than with the design motif:

Hallelujah: A Sestina

A	A wind's word, the Hebrew Hallelujah.
B	I wonder they never give it to a boy
C	(Hal for short) boy with wind-wild hair.
D	It means Praise God, as well it should since praise
E	Is what God's for. Why didn't they call my father
F	Hallelujah instead of Ebenezer?

F	Eben, of course, but christened Ebenezer,
A	Product of Nova Scotia (hallelujah).
E	Daniel, a country doctor, was his father
B	And my father his tenth and final boy.
D	A baby and last, he had a baby's praise:
C	Red petticoat, red cheeks, and crow-black hair.

C	A boy has little say about his hair
F	And little about a name like Ebenezer
D	Except that he can shorten either. Praise
A	God for that, for that shout Hallelujah.

B   Shout Hallelujah for everything a boy
E   Can be that is not his father or grandfather.

E   But then, before you know it, he is a father
C   Too and passing on his brand of hair
B   To one more perfectly defenseless boy.
F   Dubbing him John or James or Ebenezer
A   But never, so far as I know, Hallelujah,
D   As if God didn't need quite that much praise.

D   But what I'm coming to—Could I ever praise
E   My father half enough for being a father
A   Who let me be myself? Sing Hallelujah.
C   Preacher he was with a prophet's head of hair
F   And what but a prophet's name was Ebenezer,
B   However little I guessed it as a boy?

B   Outlandish names of course are never a boy's
D   Choice. And it takes time to learn to praise.
F   Stone of Help is the meaning of Ebenezer.
E   Stone of Help—what fitter name for my father?
C   Always the Stone of Help however his hair
A   Might graduate from black to Hallelujah.

BE Such is the old drama of boy and father.
DC Praise from a grayhead now with thinning hair.
FA Sing Ebenezer, Robert, sing Hallelujah!

—Robert Francis (1901–   )

The thirty-nine lines are divided into six stanzas of six lines each and a final stanza with three lines. Although no rhyming words are used, all the lines end with one of six words, each stanza following the prescribed sequence marked with capital letters; all six words appear in the final short stanza. Building such a poem requires a subject of sufficient movement or complexity to justify the length; the choice of six words that are important enough to withstand so many reuses and distinctive enough in sound to provide an interesting pattern; and the kind of writer who combines patience with a puzzle-solver's zestful search for solutions.

This sequence of forms—blank verse, the couplet, the quatrain, the sonnet, free verse, the triolet, the villanelle, and the sestina—by no means exhausts the repertoire. But it provides a helpful program for the new poet to follow in attempting to learn how forms affect the materials they organize.

Journal Projects

17. Try to write a jingle for a children's game that includes repeated words, phrases, or lines.
18. Using either trimeter or tetrameter lines, try to compose a triolet.
19. Devise two rhyming iambic pentameter lines that you think could be used as the first and third lines of a villanelle.
20. Describe in a prose paragraph some subject that is suitable for development in a sestina. Jot down those six words that might best be used for line endings.

↖ *CHOOSING A POINT OF VIEW AND A VOICE*

Imagine a person's coming upon some object that interests him, say a goldfish swimming in slow circles within a round glass bowl. The observer is visually intrigued and, if his mind has the habit of groping towards poems, he may begin to associate this picture with words and ideas in an effort to discover its total significance. Even though his search may begin in a subconscious and random way, he will, if the poem is to come to fruition, eventually make some deliberate choices in selecting a point of view and a voice for his poem.

How will the poet use his goldfish? He can describe what he sees, that is, choose the best words and form for reporting the picture. He can go further and penetrate the visible surface, suggesting the fish's motives and feelings as it swims. He can, if he wishes, emerge in the first person and concentrate on the reactions that he, the poet, has to the fish. He can use APOSTROPHE, addressing the fish as "you," as though the fish could understand. Or he can address his readers as "you," imagining their reactions to the sight. He can, for the duration of the poem, assume a new identity so that the voice of the poem belongs ostensibly to the fish rather than to the author. Obviously, the choice among these possibilities will have a major shaping effect on the poem.

Often an author chooses to stay "outside" his poem, using neither a first-person pronoun to signal his presence nor a second-person pronoun to imply a dramatic relationship with subject or reader in which he is one of the characters. "Pigeon Woman" (p. 4) is organized this way; even though the observations and words belong uniquely to May Swenson, the author is not personally within the poem. "Eight O'Clock" (p. 12) uses the same impersonal voice, but the point of view penetrates slightly beneath the surface in showing the prisoner's counting the strokes and cursing his luck. These details have been selected by the poet, but he remains aloof behind the scene.

When the poet enters the poem as "I" or as a part of "we," his open participation often increases the immediacy and the personal quality of the poem. The reader is not only shown the spider/fly/wasp drama that Edward Taylor saw ("Upon a Spider Catching a Fly," p. 36) but has it presented to him in the personalized voice of the poet, a voice that moves from playfulness to seriousness to prayer. It is interesting to notice, too, that Taylor changes his addressee in the course of the poem. He begins with apostrophe, talking directly to the spider. In the seventh stanza, though, his imperative command, *Strive not above what strength hath got,* seems to expand to include the reader for whom he is explicating a lesson. In the last two stanzas, the address is to the *mighty Gracious Lord.* This is called INVOCATION. In contrast to apostrophe, where it is obvious that the one addressed cannot receive the message, invocation assumes that the speaker believes someone to be there, usually a deity, who is able to listen.

The poet who elects to use "I" in his poem is not necessarily becoming autobiographical or even any more personal than if he chose to remain outside the poem altogether. "I" in a poem can have any of several relationships to the poet's own identity. Some poems use "I" as little more than a conventional voice, the means for making a statement. In Dobson's "A Kiss" (p. 51), the "I" speaks sentiments that might be expressed by almost anyone. The reader is aware of him most as the maker of the poem and as the man who is paying a compliment to a lady. This "I" is rather like the pronoun in such expressions as "I suppose so" or "I wonder whether it will rain."

A more intense and personal voice characterizes the "I" of "Do Not Go Gentle Into That Good Night" (p. 52). One feels keenly Dylan Thomas's unusual sensibility and response to experience. This kind of "I," the special filter for observations and feelings, the voice of everyman finely tuned to the world around him, was the frequent choice of early nineteenth-century Romantic poets. One is aware of Wordsworth or Shelley or Keats not only as makers of poems but as unique personalities partly revealed in their poetic responses to experience.

Sometimes the "I" is a fictional voice invented for the poem. Browning's Duke (p. 25) and the two speakers in "Piazza Piece" (p. 6) are fictional people, created with their own personalities, points of view, and voices, just as though they were characters in a play or novel. This device allows the author to present a double view of experience in which the reader sees the "real" event or situation and sees it again as filtered through the personality of a character whose peculiarities produce distortion. This gap between "reality" and the character's subjective view of it, delivered in a voice that may reveal more than the speaker intends, helps to define the character. The reader of "My Last Duchess" must juggle in his mind three separate considerations: what the Duchess was really like; how she seemed to her husband; and what kind of man that husband must be to hold so twisted a view.

Of increasing importance among contemporary poets is the confessional "I" who speaks the poem. Here the voice is autobiographical as in the sensitive "I" of the Romantic poets. But, while the early nineteenth-century poet typically looked at and interpreted the world of nature and experience common to all men, the modern confessional poet looks at his own unique history, reactions, and psychological configuration, creating a kind of dramatic monologue with himself as the monologist. In such a poem—and the following is a good example— the author is simultaneously his material, the interpreter of that material, and the voice that conveys the interpretation:

Lately, at Night

Father,
lately I find myself repairing
at night by inches the patchwork of your death.
The undertaker's elevator
slides upstairs like a sneak thief
going hand over hand up a back drainpipe
to an unused bedroom. The french doors open
and unction takes me by the elbow.
I am pulled up short
between those two big boys your sons, my brothers
brave as pirates putting into
a foreign port.

Tonight again
you who had sworn off funerals
and said you'd have us send out for champagne
lie stuffed and stitched like a suckling pig
prettied up for the fiesta.
Even from the doorway your profile
sticks up against air and velvet like a cutaway
springing erect in a child's pop-out book.
The jut of your nose is a thumb forced backwards.
Your eyes, those crafty Indians,
are three-quarters closed, but the twig

you wait for doesn't snap
and the old odd cleft of your chin
is faintly blue under a brand-new shave.

We whisper over you, doing business:
the middle-priced blanket of flowers,
a car to call for the reverend,
organ music to muffle the heels of all comers,
and for our mother's dizziness
two ushers to superintend.
But where are the belly dancers,
the cake that breaks open,
the whiskey and rattlers and three-corner party hats
and in this extravaganza
where is the gently tipsy old lady
who comes on at a foxtrot,
whisking you under the archway and out,
as simply as that?

I will tell them
you died with three days' whiskers on your face.
I will tell them
the final blip from the wires
daringly threaded into your heart
to keep the pace
announced itself on the radar screen
and faded down the track,
one small plane easing itself over the horizon,
and not the gas mask full of oxygen
and not the long shots of adrenalin
and nothing lusty left could haul you back.

Father,
lately at night as I watch your chest
to help it to breathe in
and swear it moves, and swear I hear the air
rising and falling,
even in the dream it is my own fat lungs

feeding themselves, greedy as ever.
Smother, drown or burn, Father,
Father, no more false moves, I beg you.
Back out of my nights, my dear dead undergroundling.
It is time. Let the pirates berth their ships,
broach casks, unload the hold, and let
the dead skin of your forehead
be a cold coin under my lips.

—Maxine Kumin (1925–   )

A comparison between this poem and "A Slumber Did My Spirit Seal" (p. 28), which is also about death and bereavement, shows how wide the gulf is between them. Here everything is individualized: the experience of a death separated from all other deaths by special detail; a reaction to death that is too complex for a simple description like "grief," "relief," "nostalgia," "resentment"; and the vehicle of expression, the voice of the poet in her role of the deceased man's haunted daughter.

Although there are several possible points of view, several "voices," for any poetic topic, a writer often has his decision made easier by the nature of his subject as he sees it and by his own temperament. The goldfish-watcher—to return to that example—who muses, "I wonder what that fish would say if he were able to communicate with me," has seen his subject in a way that includes the preference for a particular voice. This is often so. When the topic, the raw data of experience, makes its impression on an individual mind, it is shaped in the very process of being impressed; it has begun to be the poet's subject.

Among different poets (and with any poet at different times) there is temperamental variation about the willingness to enter a poem in any way that seems autobiographical. Some poets are always inside their poems; others never are; and some, conspicuously Emily Dickinson among American poets (see her "A Narrow Fellow in the Grass"), enter with a variety of slight disguises. The poet who is somewhat reticent about announcing subjective ideas as his own may elect to stay outside the poem altogether. One who wants to emphasize his special view and his own feelings will more willingly make himself evident. Obviously, only the poet who does not strongly resist a certain measure of self-exposure is capable of writing in the confessional "I." Although there is no rule that writing a poem should be a comfortable experience, it is often a good idea to choose the point of view that seems least to violate the poet's own sense of his place vis-à-vis his subject and his reader.

JOURNAL PROJECTS

21. Return to Project #13, the subjects for which you considered suitable forms. As you think about each of these, jot down the point(s) of view you think would be most appropriate for expressing your own sense of the subject.
22. Contemplate some item in your environment (a piece of furniture, an animal or plant, a book or painting, etc.). Using whatever form you wish, write three short poems about that item with the following points of view:
    a. Impersonal, the poet outside the poem altogether.
    b. Personal, the poet entering in his own identity to whatever degree he wishes.
    c. The fictional "I," where the item is given the voice of the poem.
23. Try to begin a poem using the confessional "I," being careful to record whatever feelings of release or resistance you encounter in the process.
24. Look again at your sonnet (Project #12) and your persuasive poem in free verse (Projects #7, #16). Consider the point of view and the voice in each. Have you made the best choices? Would a change improve either poem?

EXPERIMENTING WITH UNUSUAL FORMS

Much of the discussion about form thus far has rested on the assumption that the metric foot is the basic unit from which lines and poems are made. That is an oversimplification. The idea of the metric foot was devised after the fact by people who wanted to talk about existing poetry. Poems were composed before metric measure was a familiar concept; indeed they are still being composed by people who know nothing of the theory of metrics. Most contemporary writers, whether instinctively or by design, use rhythms that can be described in terms of the metric foot. But some distinguished poets do not write that way, and it is important for every writer to realize that there are alternatives.

Gerard Manley Hopkins, though chronologically a Victorian, may well be called the first of the modern poets. He used what he called SPRUNG RHYTHM in much of his work. This was an effort to evade the restraints of METRIC STRESS in favor of the SENSE STRESS rhythms that characterize pre-Spenserian English poetry and have had a continuous history in children's rhymes, jingles, and the lyrics of popular songs. Sprung rhythm takes no account of iambs or trochees or the counting of syllables or divisions of the line into metric feet, but concentrates instead on the number of stresses or beats to the line. If a

three-beat line is selected, that line contains three stressed
syllables; these follow each other consecutively or are separated
by one, two, three, or four unstressed syllables, however many
would be needed by the words required for sense. This can
be illustrated simply in many popular nursery rhymes:

> Pease porridge hot,
> Pease porridge cold,
> Pease porridge in the pot
> Nine days old.

One could describe these lines metrically, but only with much
troublesome patching and piecing. And the resulting description would not be "right." Anyone who's ever recited them
knows that there are three large beats or stresses to each
line, no matter what a metrical scanner might say. What is
more, each line takes the same time to say, whether it has
six syllables like the third or three syllables like the fourth.
The times between stresses are equal, no matter how many or
how few unstressed syllables fill them up. This is comparable
to the situation in music. Each common measure in a musical
composition uses up the same time, whether it contains one
whole note or four quarter notes or eight eighth notes or any
possible combination of notes and rests. Numbers of notes are
not significant; and, in sprung rhythm, the numbers of syllables, so useful in metrical stress, are not significant. One can
see the effect that this rhythm has on a serious poem in this
curtal sonnet:

Pied Beauty

Glory be to God for dappled things—
　　For skies of couple-colour as a brinded cow;
　　　　For rose-moles all in stipple upon trout that swim;
Fresh-firecoal chestnut-falls; finches' wings;

> Landscape plotted and pieced—fold, fallow, and plough;
>> And all trades, their gear and tackle and trim.
>
> All things counter, original, spare, strange;
>> Whatever is fickle, freckled (who knows how?)
>>> With swift, slow; sweet, sour; adazzle, dim;
> He fathers-forth whose beauty is past change:
>>>> Praise him.

>>>>> —Gerard Manley Hopkins (1844–1889)

Reading these lines aloud, one tends to give five stresses to each of the ten full lines; but it would be folly to cite the iamb or any other foot as dominant or even to talk too seriously about pentameter.

Another way of writing with sense stress deserves attention because it has attracted some distinguished contemporary writers. Verse patterns can be successfully devised that take into account only gross numbers of syllables, without regard for counting stresses. Here is an example:

To a Steam Roller

The illustration
is nothing to you without the application.
> You lack half wit. You crush all the particles down
>> into close conformity, and then walk back and forth on them.

Sparkling chips of rock
are crushed down to the level of the parent block.
> Were not "impersonal judgment in aesthetic
>> matters, a metaphysical impossibility," you

might fairly achieve
it. As for butterflies, I can hardly conceive
> of one's attending upon you, but to question
>> the congruence of the complement is vain, if it exists.

>>> —Marianne Moore (1887–   )

Certainly there is pattern here. Each stanza is meticulously constructed of four lines, the first line with five syllables, the second and third with twelve each, the fourth with fifteen. But lines of comparable count are scarcely of comparable rhythm. Consider these three, each marked for stress as one might read it aloud according to its sense:

> The illustration
> Sparkling chips of rock
> might fairly achieve

The poem designed by syllabic count makes possible a combination not available in most poetry—the organization of verse form, plus the prose writer's freedom from constraints that most verse forms impose. Probably no poem in metric-stress rhythm could incorporate the learned quotation that "To a Steam Roller" contains because the words and their arrangement don't fit any meter.

A variety of syllabic poetry that has recently found favor with writers of English poetry is the HAIKU, a centuries-old Japanese verse form. Since English is a very different language from Japanese, and since the cultural patterns of English-speaking people are not like those of Orientals, a *haiku* necessarily suffers a sea change when it is composed in English. But, formally at least, it can simulate the Japanese pattern, which requires that the poem consist of seventeen syllables in three lines, five in the first and third, seven in the second. The Japanese have some firm customs about appropriate subject and tone for this form that many writers in English also attempt to observe. The *haiku* should refer to one of the seasons, either explicitly or by the inclusion of some natural detail that represents a season. The *haiku* typically uses concrete description to evoke a mood, and that mood is suggested to the reader rather than developed in words. Thus, a short description of the first robin in a garden just losing its winter snow would convey a sense of spring's beginning and a mood of hopeful anticipation. Here are two *haiku* written by Americans:

> A long chain of geese
>   measures the gray sky from north
>   to south . . . days shorten
>
>> —Eva Gorham Craig
>
> The skaters have gone—
>   leaving the moon's reflection
>   frozen in scratched ice.
>
>> —Gustave Keyser

It is difficult to write a *haiku* that is precise in form and effective in subtly conveying meaning, but the disciplines of choosing words and counting syllables are helpful for the beginner poet.

Among contemporary poets in Europe and America, there are many who experiment with new ways of searching for form. One such way culminates in what is called FOUND POETRY. A found poem puts into poetic shape, usually into a free-verse stanza, some sequence of words that was not intended as poetry. The hunter on the trail of likely sequences becomes a close reader of relish labels, do-it-yourself instruction pamphlets, advertising copy, dust-jacket testimonials, and news reports. When he finds a phrase, sentence, or longer passage that seems to have rhythm or some other arresting sound effect, he sets it down in a series of lines to look like a piece of poetry. Here, set as found poetry, are the verbatim remarks of a high school teacher, talking to some colleagues about technical procedures for staging a school play:

Know the ways of working with simple things:
Don't go overboard on something
That is way out of reach.

You've got to know your stage,
Your wattage, what the stage can carry;
Work out the lighting so you don't

Burn out the wires or cause a short.
In case of emergency, know where your exits are,
Know when to put the house lights on.

Try to get the green boys and break them in.
So you have to break a few rules,
        How else can you be creative?

Although it is rare to find a sequence that makes a formal poem, this is sometimes possible:

Hence no force, however great,
Can stretch a cord, however fine,
Into a horizontal line,
Which is accurately straight.

Written as prose, this observation appeared in *An Elementary Treatise on Mechanics* by the Reverend William Whewell, an early nineteenth-century teacher of mathematics, mineralogy, and moral theology at Cambridge University. A few years after its publication, Adam Sedgwick, a celebrated geologist, recited these lines as poetry in the course of an after-dinner speech. Whewell was not amused and changed the wording in the next edition to prevent the rediscovery of a found poem within his learned treatise.

In "finding" poetry, most of the effort goes into the search for prose that has enough rhythm or repetition of sounds to justify an artistic arrangement. The act of arranging is relatively simple, usually governed by lines set to emphasize comparable sounds and to encourage a rhythmic reading. There is an ironic delight in coming upon a pleasing pattern in words meant to give information rather than pleasure. If this element of surprise is strong enough, it can compensate for some lack of depth in meaning and for vocabulary that would seem unremarkable in other contexts. One judges found poetry by its own set of standards. Material that a writer would reject as trite or humdrum for a made poem may seem pleasing when he discovers it embedded in ordinary prose where he is astonished to find anything that resembles poetry at all. Found poetry is like pop art in its assertion of artistic value for what is usually considered merely functional.

The term CONCRETE POETRY designates poems in which the arrangement of typography and other symbols helps to make the meaning. It may be useful to talk first and separately about one special variety of the concrete poem. The SHAPED POEM is not a contemporary innovation but is at least as old as George Herbert's work in the early seventeenth century. This sort of poem involves the kind of verbal sense typical of more conventional poetry together with an unusual placement of individual words and lines to simulate a shape. In Herbert's "Easter Wings," for example, the two rhymed stanzas look like a pair of wings.

One might say that the shaped poem is an extended thrust of the effort to find a suitable form for an idea. In more conventional poetry, the writer searching for form chooses among familiar possibilities involving the length of lines and stanzas; the emphasis is on form that will appropriately enclose meaning and will emphasize any pattern of rhythm or sound that a poem contains. In the shaped poem, the look of the work on the page is more important than rhythm or sound, and the form not only encloses but also represents meaning. In this modern example, "A Weaver of Carpets" by Sam Toperoff, the lines are put into an elaborate visual pattern that suggests a Persian rug.

A WEAVER OF CARPETS

The
eternal
truth of my father's
words I have come to know:
"The Piety of Imperfection is the
greatest burden of all."
I, Mahmoud, have
found it
so.
When
I was a young
man at my craft, Im-
perfection was the seed
of all my art. Allah alone could
form a perfect thing, so,
as all must do, in my
carpets
I
wove
The Sacred Error
which more than satisfied
the letter of His Holy Law, but
with experience I wove a central flaw
which, somehow, all but pleased
those very holy eyes
it set about to
tease.
My
tapestries were much in demand throughout the
kingdom. Un-
like the
dolts
who hid The
Sacred Error in
the border or in the
Arabesque (brave souls!), I
left ragged the very
cheetah's claw
that should
have
curled
around the
Caliph's daughter.
In limitation I found
the source of strength . . . and a
liberal fee as well,
while my rep-
utation
grew.
But the
critics couldn't
be pleased. At first
they cried, "How brazen is
this Mahmoud to flaunt his Frailty
so."
And now
when I, the Mas-
ter, drop a border stitch
or two, they chide, "No longer
certain, eh Mahmoud?
No arrogance
to show us
any-
more?"
They think
I've fallen into
line and left my Pride in
a corner place. They do not know
Mahmoud. Each evening
I weave a flower pat-
tern, a Holy
Car-
pet, which
I shall leave to
the Mosque at Ardebil.
It shall be flawless! Quite
perfect! My father's words are
hidden in the cartouche,
for I am, first,
a weaver
of car-
pets.

—Sam Toperoff (1933–   )

To listen to a shaped poem without seeing the text is to lose at least half of its value.

With other kinds of concrete poetry, all the value is lost when the poem cannot be seen. In contrast to shaped poems like "A Weaver of Carpets," most experiments in concrete poetry forgo normal syntactical arrangement as a method for conveying meaning. Words, and sometimes other symbols too, are used as components in a design. Visual arrangement replaces the logic of grammar and punctuation, and the point of the poem is lodged in the pattern, a collage of individual symbols. The following example by a contemporary German poet looks like an apple shape cut from a repeated pattern of the German word for "apple":

—Reinhard Döhl (1934–   )

Those who contemplate this poem might be called viewers rather than readers, since the process they engage in resembles the one used for looking at a picture. Close attention is required, however, if one is not to miss the "trick" of this poem, the *Wurm* (worm) in the lower righthand corner of the apple. Another example, by Jane Poston (1923–   ), combines a repeated command with a typographical representation of the effects of that command:

stay in line
stay in line

stay in line

stay in line
stay in line

stay in line

stay in line
stay in line

stay in line

stay in line
stay in line

stay in line

stay in line
stay in line

stay in line

stay in line
stay in line

stay in line

stay in line
stay in line

stay in line

stay in line
stay in line

stay in line

stay in line
stay in line

stay in line

stay in line
stay in line

stay in line

stay in line
stay in line

stay in line

stay in line
stay in line

fowl
flap
fling
swing
wing
water
wave
wash
swish
fish

Sky and Water / by Maurits C. Escher, collection of C.V.S. Roosevelt, Washington, D.C.

Those for whom poetry implies the sense achieved through the usual interrelationships of words may find concrete poetry thin, unprofitably bizarre. This poetry needs to be judged by different standards, as an effort to work in that largely unexploited area where printed words and pictures come together and where the conveyance of meaning is intimately shared between them. Marshall McLuhan might cite the concrete poem as a move away from the linearity of printed messages towards the graphic communications that an era of film has encouraged. Perhaps the connection between words and the graphic arts can best be illustrated in the example on the preceding page.

JOURNAL PROJECTS

25. Try to write four *haiku,* one for each of the four seasons.
26. Read a copy of your daily newspaper or a popular magazine slowly and completely, including all advertisements. Copy any sequences that suggest the possibility of a found poem. Can any one of these sequences be arranged so as to emphasize rhythm, comparable sounds, or both?

WORKING WITH WORDS

CHOOSING WORDS

Whatever the subject, whatever the ideological or emotional content, whatever the form, a poem ultimately depends on its individual words. Vocabulary that is vague or inappropriate or poor in connotative quality can stifle even the most engaging theme or the most potent feeling. Conversely, a small or long-familiar subject can, through the author's meticulous choice of words, be shaped into a memorable poem.

The words for poems are not chosen as they are for expository prose. In prose, the first consideration is likely to be clarity; the writer strives to select those words that will convey his meaning to a reader directly and without confusion. Clarity is needed for poetry, too, but it is often not the most important criterion. Indeed, there are occasions when the ambiguous, the puzzling word is deliberately selected instead of a more direct synonym in order to enrich the poem. As a practicing poet becomes more and more sensitive to individual words, his sense of the "right" vocabulary increases. He gains confidence about selecting words that fit his feeling about the subject and the way he wants his reader to react.

Most competent poets adopt a certain level of formality in words and consistently maintain it. The same is true of prose communications, both written and oral, where the choice of level comes so naturally that it is often automatic. Consider the following ways of inviting someone to the theatre:

1. You are invited to attend a performance of *Hamlet* on Wednesday evening, May 21st, at the Orpheum Theatre. Curtain at 8:30.
2. Can you join us to see *Hamlet* next Wednesday evening at the Orpheum? The play begins at 8:30.
3. How about going to *Hamlet* with us at the Orpheum Wednesday? Can you make it by 8:30?

These invitations are identical in subject and purpose. The vocabulary in which each is expressed, though, conveys other kinds of information—how well the host knows his guest, how intimate the theatre party is likely to be, how much advance planning has preceded the invitation. The invited person would respond differently to each. In a similar way, the level of formality that a writer chooses for the words of his poem conveys information about his feelings for the subject and the reaction he wants his reader to have to the poem. Each of these two poems recounts the suicide of a man of property, but they are characterized by different levels of vocabulary:

Richard Cory

Whenever Richard Cory went down town,
We people on the pavement looked at him:
He was a gentleman from sole to crown,
Clean favored, and imperially slim.

And he was always quietly arrayed,
And he was always human when he talked;
But still he fluttered pulses when he said,
"Good morning," and he glittered when he walked.

And he was rich—yes, richer than a king—
And admirably schooled in every grace:
In fine, we thought that he was everything
To make us wish that we were in his place.

So on we worked, and waited for the light,
And went without the meat, and cursed the bread;
And Richard Cory, one calm summer night,
Went home and put a bullet through his head.

—Edwin Arlington Robinson (1869–1935)

American Primitive

Look at him there in his stovepipe hat,
His high-top shoes, and his handsome collar;
Only my Daddy could look like that,
And I love my Daddy like he loves his Dollar.

The screen door bangs, and it sounds so funny,
There he is in a shower of gold;
His pockets are stuffed with folding money,
His lips are blue, and his hands feel cold.

He hangs in the hall by his black cravat,
The ladies faint, and the children holler:
Only my Daddy could look like that,
And I love my Daddy like he loves his Dollar.

—William Jay Smith (1918–   )

"Richard Cory" uses a vocabulary that is mostly in the middle range, neither extremely formal nor colloquial. Expressions like *down town, pavement, richer than a king, went without the meat, one calm summer night* are drawn from the language of people speaking informally but with a sense of propriety that precludes much colloquialism. "American Primitive," on the other hand, uses a colloquial vocabulary including *Daddy, like* (for "as"), *funny* (meaning "peculiar"), *folding money, holler*. In each poem, the level chosen gives useful information about the speaker and his attitude to the suicide and guides a reader's feelings towards a specific reaction. The voice that tells the story of Richard Cory belongs to an ordinary towns-

man of simple dignity who is impressed with the irony of the
event. The reader will probably appreciate this irony too, and
will have feelings that combine pity for Richard Cory, a
wonder at the secret anguish beneath a fortunate exterior, a
fresh realization of the difference between the way things seem
and the way they really are. The voice in "American Primitive" belongs to a young person who seems not fully to comprehend the significance of his father's death, either because of
youth or lack of sensitivity. The reader is likely to react with
less sympathy than to the death of Richard Cory, to say to
himself, "Well, when a person is too mercenary, he'll probably
come to a bad end."

For most poems, maintaining a single level of language is
the best procedure. But both "Richard Cory" and "American
Primitive" show that mixing levels can sometimes be useful.
When the speaker of the first poem slides into rather erudite
expressions like *imperially, arrayed, admirably schooled, in
fine,* he is casting an aura of regal authority upon Richard
Cory, using the words an average man might summon to
describe or address his superior. These excursions out of the
informal to a more formal vocabulary are purposeful. In
"American Primitive," *cravat* is also quite deliberate. The
speaker might have been expected to use *tie* or *necktie* as the
companion for *stovepipe hat*. What does the more elegant word
add to the poem's meaning? Perhaps it suggests the pretentious diction of the newly rich money-maker who, as his wealth
increases, adopts a few French words for everyday items.
Words like *imperially* and *arrayed* would be intrusions in this
poem, but *cravat* is a useful borrowing from a more formal
vocabulary. For any poem, the words ought to belong to the
same level unless an inconsistent selection entails advantages.

Aside from the three obvious levels of language—formal,
informal, and colloquial—the new poet should be aware of
a fourth class of vocabulary that can be called "bizarre," pro-

vided no pejorative sense is attached to that adjective. The bizarre vocabulary includes words of the poet's own invention or uses standard expressions in ways that violate custom. Lewis Carroll's "Jabberwocky" is largely composed of lines like these:

> 'Twas brillig, and the slithy toves
> Did gyre and gimble in the wabe . . .

One recognizes a few words that the dictionary can derive and define, but most have been coined by the author. A reader, though, can usually ascertain a meaning quite easily. It is remarkable to discover how much general agreement there is about the meanings of *slithy* (*slippery* + *lithe*) and *gimble* (*gambol* + *nimble*). Words made up for a poem always run the risk of seeming arch and self-consciously clever. Some inventions, though, succeed because the sounds are delightful and amusing, as they are in "Jabberwocky." One feels that, if *brillig* and *gimble* were not part of the language, Lewis Carroll did well to bring them in. Coined words can have another purpose too. Reading the whole of "Jabberwocky," with its many invented nouns, verbs, and adjectives, one still gets the sense of a complete story. The author has demonstrated vividly that English, like other languages, includes large measures of redundancy, that a significant percentage of any communication can be turned into nonsense without obliterating the message. When a poet wishes to underscore the fact that an event or scene is predictable because it follows a familiar pattern, the use of nonsense words may help him to emphasize that idea.

Along with coining words, poets frequently assume the right to make their own designations of parts of speech. The reader who encounters E. E. Cummings's line, *but if a look should april me,* may begin by protesting that the months of the year

are nouns, and proper nouns at that. Further attention to the
poem, though, may persuade even the purist that *april* is a
rich and forceful verb in the context. It suggests the sudden
conferring of a springlike vigor and freshness upon *me,* and
does it with a single word.

Some writers of poetry, and some readers too, hold strong
prejudices about the nature of vocabulary that is suitable,
much as though English included a special and limited sub-
division of words appropriate to poetic expression. One sometimes hears "That's too vulgar for poetry" about the poem
that uses plain language, colloquialisms, or slang. At the opposite pole are those who insist that any words not drawn
from the simple, sometimes salty, speech of everyday usage
are unnaturally pretentious. Some suppose that multi-syllabic
words from Latin roots are too cerebral and unfeeling for
poetry; others say that an unadorned and simple vocabulary
lacks style. Between those who want eagles to be called *big
birds* and those who insist on *majestic pinioned coursers of
the air* there is likely to be little ground for compromise.

It is undoubtedly wisest to begin with the assumption that
no words are unsuitable for poetry generally, but that any
word may be unsuitable for a particular poem. The whole
vocabulary is the poet's field, and his is the burden of sifting
out good choices. The selection is best made not on the basis
of which word is "most poetic" but which carries the meaning, the feeling, and the tone that the poem requires.

Even though there are no valid limits except the needs of
his poem to constrict a poet's search for words, he ought to be
wary of expressions that may bore or annoy a reader because they are "over-poetic." Usually these are drawn from
older styles of poetry and, like bad habits that cannot easily
be broken, for some poets they remain attached to the whole
process of writing poems.

Certain contractions comprise one such class of expressions.

During eras when meter was more strictly observed than now, *'tis, 'twere, wouldst, 'gainst, o'er, morn,* etc., were convenient for compressing two syllables into one so as not to roughen the line. Modern poetry is less disturbed by metrical irregularity, and most readers now would prefer an extra syllable to a contraction that is archaic and uselessly artificial. Those contractions in current use, however, such as *can't, don't, wouldn't,* and *isn't,* remain suitable for poetry except at a very formal level of language, where the uncontracted form would normally be more appropriate.

Thou, thee, and *thy* have had a remarkable endurance. Long after their place in prose had given way to *you* and *your,* they survived in the practice of poetry. The Victorian poet who probably never put these terms to use in prose writing or speech, except for addressing the deity, continued to write poetry as though they were appropriate. Strangely, the tendency still persists among some poets, as though the writing of poems required a shift of gears into an older style. In contemporary poetry, except for prayers, hymns, or efforts to simulate the language of a special time or region, these forms are disconcerting affectations.

It was a custom with some eighteenth-century poets to put familiar nouns in fancy dress, probably to make them more interesting. This typically involved using several words for one, and the pattern still has some adherents. To refer to fish as *the finny breed,* to birds as *feathered warblers,* to bees as *denizens of the hive* now seems unproductively evasive and abstract. The extra words do not add aesthetic value or meaning; in fact, they subtract quantities of both.

Perhaps the most lamentable addiction of the inexperienced poet is his appetite for flowery language. In his eagerness to be vivid and to make certain that his reader receives a complete description, the new poet often piles up modifiers for his nouns and verbs, supposing that meaning will be enhanced in proportion to an increase in syllables and words. The experienced poet knows better; meaning is often swamped in excess vocabulary, but is made clear and forceful through the careful choice of the fewest and best words. Adjectives and adverbs are respectable parts of speech, but a poem is usually stronger if they are used sparingly. Whenever a specific verb can be made to do the work of a general verb and its adverb (e.g. *crept* or *ambled* for *walked slowly*), whenever a specific noun can do the work of a general noun and its adjective (e.g. *feast* or *banquet* for *large, delicious dinner*), the substitution should be seriously considered. Modern tastes are less tolerant of modifiers than those of former years. Reading Thomas Gray's famous poem, "Elegy Written in a Country Churchyard," one becomes increasingly irritated by the modifiers in every line. The effect, in these times when sparer, leaner language is preferred, may be heavy, monotonous.

Probably a poet's most time-consuming and tantalizing pursuit is the search for exactly the right word in a tangle of near-right possibilities. He may know that he needs a noun to convey the idea of light that is muted rather than intense. Words like *lustre, glow, sheen* come to mind. If he hunts more rigorously, he may discover *shimmer, gloss, radiance, glimmer, glint, phosphorescence, luminescence, iridescence, gleam*. If he is lucky, the word he needs is one of these and he will recognize it. But he may be dissatisfied with all of them and be obliged to probe further both his mind and his thesaurus.

Used carefully, a good thesaurus can be an invaluable assistant to any writer. This stockpile of words and phrases groups its entries according to the ideas they express. If one were to look up *lustre* in the thesaurus index, one would be referred to a section containing a large collection of words having to do with all qualities of light, subdivided according to the various parts of speech. By combing these lists, a poet may hit upon exactly the right word for his purpose. He must, of course, first know the kind of idea he is striving to verbalize so that he can use the thesaurus index effectively. And he cannot depend on the thesaurus alone because it contains no precise definitions or aids for distinguishing among words with similar meanings. The writer who thinks he's found his word in a thesaurus should next check its meaning in the dictionary to be sure that his understanding of it is accurate.

Aside from considerations of sound, to be discussed later, a poet selects his word on the basis of its total meaning. The qualifying "total" is important, signifying not only the bare definition of the word but also the meanings that attend that word in use. The word *ilk,* for example, originally meant "same," and by extension, "kind" or "family." This is the unadorned, basic definition of ilk, or its DENOTATION. But by usage in this country now, *ilk* is usually pejorative and signifies the user's contempt for the group he is talking about. The CONNOTATIONS of *ilk* are unfavorable and involve disapproval, contempt, disdain. A writer would not use the word in speaking of a family or kind that he wants his reader to admire or respect. Tactful people are sensitive to the connotative qualities of words they use. Someone who seeks to compliment a woman refers to her as *petite* rather than *undersized* or *puny* if she is short and thin; as *stately* or *statuesque* rather than *big* or *horsy* if she is tall and muscular. The retailer marketing a red dress may name its color *apple, cardinal, scarlet, flame,* or *ruby.* If he were to call it *blood, borscht,* or *radish* he would sell fewer dresses.

To observe how a poet uses connotations in choosing words, it will be helpful to turn back to Robert Frost's poem, "Design" (p. 41). One of its arresting phrases is *witches' broth* (line 6). The more usual expression is certainly *witches' brew,* the connotations of which are all unpleasant. Why does Frost use *broth* instead? An obvious reason is for its rhyme. But conspicuous among Frost's excellences is his ability to rhyme without compromising word choices; one can depend on his having also chosen *broth* because of some value in its total meaning. *Broth* has several pleasant connotations—nourishment, warmth, comfort in illness, "a broth of a boy." Combined with *witches'*, it gives the total expression ambiguous value, both unpleasant and pleasant. But isn't that typical of values throughout the poem, where the speaker seems undecided whether the scene is a natural, pretty coincidence or the result of some evil design?

An earlier version of the poem included the word *dented* instead of *dimpled* (line 1). As far as the spider's appearance is concerned, both words describe indentions on his body. *Dented*, though, has unfavorable connotations, suggesting things that have been bumped and marred, like fenders. Reactions to *dimpled*, on the contrary, are usually positive because the word suggests a pleasant feature in the appearance of some persons, especially babies. Again Frost has created an ambiguous expression—*dimpled spider*—in which the first word has positive value, the second neutral or negative value; together they emphasize the ambiguity of the poem's idea.

Connotations that adhere to a word most often involve feelings and attitudes. Sometimes, though, the extra, hovering value is one that appeals to the mind rather than the emotions. Frost's *innocent* (line 10) is an example. The reader encountering this word in other places usually selects one of several meanings, depending on the context, the material surrounding the word. It may mean "helpless" or "unsuspecting" (an innocent victim), or "uninvolved" (an innocent bystander), or "not guilty" (of a crime), or "simple," "ingenuous," "unsophisticated" (an innocent baby, child, girl). Nagging the consciousness of anyone who's studied Latin, however, is the original, root meaning of *innocent*, that is, "not harmful." The whole question of "harm" vs. "harmless" is reinforced through this word. Does the harmless blue flower become harmful when white? Or is the flower harmless regardless of color except when made the agent of a harmful plan? Is the whole scene a harmless coincidence or a harmful portent? The word raises the same unanswered questions as the frequent references to the color white. Does white connote purity and innocence, or bloodlessness, ghosts, and death?

The sound of a word can sometimes be the source of connotative overtones. Frost's *appall* (line 13) provides an example. Derived from a root meaning "to grow or make pale" (certainly a good choice for this white design), the meaning is now usually "to overwhelm or discourage with fear or horror," a meaning also suitable for the poem. But the sound of the word can scarcely fail to suggest *pall,* and the meaning of *pall* ("a cloth put over a coffin," or "the coffin itself") becomes part of the connotative overtone for *appall.* Since *cloth* and *death* are both mentioned elsewhere in the poem, these connotations are rich and appropriate.

One could cite several other examples in this poem of words chosen because their connotations are more consistent with the poem's controlling idea than alternate choices would have been—*rigid* instead of *stiff* or *lifeless; froth* instead of *foam* or *meringue; kindred* instead of *same-colored* or *near* or *related; steered* instead of *led, pushed, pulled, directed.* Together, all of these choices form a kind of connotative network that runs through the poem, a network of ambiguities to reinforce the large *If* of the final line.

JOURNAL PROJECTS

27. Using whatever form you like, write a short poem with the same theme as "Delight in Disorder" (p. 26), but using a more informal, perhaps even a colloquial, vocabulary.
28. List all possible words you can think of or find in your thesaurus that mean the coming together of more than two people (e.g.

convention). Using a dictionary, establish the denotative meaning of each. Then list any connotative values you associate with
each word.

29. For each of the following words of neutral value, think of at
    least two comparable words, one with negative connotations and
    one with positive connotations (e.g. *large—gross, grand*): *girl,
    house, horse, to speak, to plan, warm, quiet, old, difficult, con-
    tinually, quickly.*

30. Return to your sonnet (Projects #12, #24) and your persua-
    sive poem in free verse (Projects #7, #16, #24) to examine
    vocabulary closely. In each poem are your words drawn from
    about the same level of formality? If there are exceptions, are
    these purposeful? Does either poem contain archaic or flowery
    language that ought to be changed? Can you reduce the number
    of modifiers without loss to the meaning of either poem? Can
    you enrich connotative quality anywhere by changes in words?

ARRANGING WORDS

A prose writer arranges his words according to the conventions of syntax. He writes in sentences that usually contain a subject and a predicate. His adjectives typically precede the nouns they modify. Statements that are subordinate to a sentence's main idea are put into dependent clauses. To make the message clearer, he uses certain conventional punctuation marks. A sentence begins with a capital letter and ends with a period. Commas separate some clauses and the items in a series. And so forth.

Whether he chooses to conform to them or to violate them completely, the poet must be always aware of these conventions because they are part of his reader's equipment for understanding things in print. But the poet's criteria for arranging words are much more complex. He has to consider not only the general unit, the sentence, but also a special unit, his own line of verse. The tension between sentence and line, between the conventions of syntax and the demands of metrical or syllabic form, is both a burden and an opportunity. Howard Nemerov's "The Map-Maker on His Art" (p. 21) is written in sentences all correct enough to satisfy a grammarian. But the poem is also written in iambic pentameter lines. At some points, where the lines are end-stopped, there is a momentary correspondence between syntax and meter;

in other places, line and sentence are not in phase but are contrapuntal, and the reader finds this counterpoint interesting.

There are times when meter or sound or idea demands that the poet depart from normal syntax or neglect it completely, and he exercises what is called his POETIC LICENSE. This simply means permission to break the usual rules for the sake of some artistic effect, and poets are constantly availing themselves of the privilege. It has already been noted, for example, that the second stanza of Whitman's "A Noiseless Patient Spider" (p. 39) is an incomplete sentence; there is a subject and the subject is modified by various participles, but there is no principal verb. A teacher of prose composition would probably mark the whole thing "Fragment!" But Whitman's idea of incomplete effort is gracefully emphasized by this incomplete sentence.

Robert Herrick's "Delight in Disorder" (p. 26) incorporates an arrangement that a prose writer might avoid. Lines 3 through 12 contain five sentence subjects; only after all five have been listed, and each modified in some detail, does one reach the predicate verb. The prose writer would probably worry about his reader's losing the thread of such a sentence, but, in this poem, the tetrameter couplets provide a neat pattern through which a reader can proceed easily. That part of the predicate, *do more bewitch me,* is itself a departure from normal expression. One would be inclined to say *bewitch me more* in prose, but the metric pattern calls for the less usual arrangement. Poets frequently invert the normal order of words in the interests of rhyme and meter, and, unless such inversion seems forced, unless the reader is painfully aware that logical sequences are being wrenched out of shape to make them fit the form, it is quite acceptable. Unskilled poets often affect unnecessary inversions in order to sound poetic, and they succeed only in making their lines trite and artificial. Many of the best twentieth-century poems use a syntax that is like the syntax of prose.

The poet is free to be ungrammatical if his poem requires it and provided he does not obscure his idea. In the second stanza of Emily Dickinson's "The Soul Selects" (p. 28), the words, *an Emperor be kneeling/Upon her Mat,* make it impossible to parse the sentence. If they are the object of *she notes,* they are a very strange object indeed. Or perhaps one should infer *may* before *be,* or *even though* before *an.* One cannot decide among these possibilities, but no decision is required. The meaning is entirely clear. The punctuation of the poem is bizarre, in accordance with the author's usual preference. Capital letters not only begin the lines of poetry, but they are used to begin most of the nouns, presumably to focus attention upon these key words. The only stop indicators are dashes. For prose uses, this would seem chaotic. But, if the poem is thought of as something to be read aloud, dashes are sufficient to mark pauses; the voice can make little distinction among commas, semicolons, and periods.

Contemporary poets cover a wide spectrum of practices in the way they punctuate. The old custom of using capital letters to begin all sentences and all lines is no longer universal. Some poets use the capital only for beginning a sentence (see "Pigeon Woman," p. 4). Some poets, notably E. E. Cummings, scarcely use it at all except for an occasional important noun in the middle of a sentence. And some like to put a whole word in caps to accentuate it. There is similar diversity in respect to marks for pauses. Some poets follow the rules of prose. Others use a bare minimum of marks, letting line endings and breaks between stanzas indicate pauses. Still others avoid marks entirely. It does not matter what system of punctuation a poem employs so long as it is intentional and so long as the meaning is clear.

Poetic license confers tremendous freedom upon the writer, but it also confers large responsibilities. Unusual syntax and punctuation ought to serve a purpose, to be meaningful departures from convention rather than arch attempts to be different.

In arranging the words of a poem, most poets most of the time keep two considerations in mind—how the poem looks on the page and how the poem sounds when read aloud. When the writer deals with decisions concerning length of line, stanza breaks, indentations, and all matters that affect typography, he is thinking about making his poem meaningful to a reader. When he occupies himself with rhythm, rhyme, and the way words sound individually or in sequence, he is thinking about making his poem meaningful to a listener. Usually he does both simultaneously.

Poetry was originally composed to be heard, but, through the centuries, the look of the poem on the page has become increasingly important. More people now have opportunities to read poems than to hear them being read, so vision is more important than sound. This probably accounts for the startling contemporary thrust towards visual effects, culminating in the concrete poem. The typewriter, now part of the working equipment of almost all writers, both amateur and professional, has inspired experiments with textual arrangement that would probably not have occurred to poets writing by hand. It is regrettable that, in many cases, the innovations do not seem worthwhile. Catching the reader's eye with devices that have no appropriateness, that lead nowhere, is a sterile pastime. On the other hand, when a unique arrangement enhances the sense of the poem or suggests relationships that a reader might otherwise have missed, the effect can be valuable, as in this poem by E. E. Cummings (1894–1962):

                                        un
                                        der fog
                                        's
                                        touch

                                slo

                                        ings
                                        fin
                                        gering
                                        s

                                wli

                                        whichs
                                        turn
                                        in
                                        to whos

                                est

                                        people
                                        be
                                        come
                                        un

Obviously, no one could read this poem aloud; indeed, it takes some ingenuity to read it on the page. Once the idea comes through, though, it is clear that the unusual arrangement of syllables is purposeful and interesting. An invented adverb, divided into thirds, forms a left-hand column. It is not very difficult to ascertain that its relationship to the rest of the text is that of a modifier, describing the manner in which the other actions take place. Those other actions, divided into very short lines and stanzas, are the changes fog makes in the appearances of things it encloses. All this is strung out, almost syllable by syllable, to show how gradual the changes are. The final syllable's likeness to the first suggests a circular motion in which the process begins again; *un* means both "not" and the first syllable of *under*. The arrangement is certainly strange but not strange for strangeness's sake. The placement of type not only emphasizes but partly makes the meaning.*

Unlike this poem about fog, the majority of poems in English include sound devices that seek to buttress the poem's meaning or to increase the poem's aesthetic appeal. Rhythm, an arrangement of stressed and unstressed syllables that is somewhat predictable, is the most pervasive of the means for achieving sound effects. Whether a writer uses iambic pentameter because he has the urge to write a sonnet, whether he chooses it because that rhythm seems to suit his subject, or whether the words he writes just seem to fall into iambic pentameter lines, the pattern becomes a part of his poem that affects both the developing subject and the reader's reaction.

Poems in free verse can also make use of rhythm. When Walt Whitman's "A Noiseless Patient Spider" (p. 39) is read aloud, a recurrent rhythm that suggests elongation and repetition is evident. It is interesting to contrast the sound of this poem with Marianne Moore's "To a Steam Roller." The latter has a more regular form, but the form is shaped by syllabic count without a stress pattern, and the poem is not rhythmic.

Various metric feet and various line lengths have their own moods that help to make meaning. Consider, for example, this one of "Seven Double Dactyls" by George Starbuck (1931–   ):

Said

Agatha Christie to
E. Phillips Oppenheim,

---

* Readers who would like to read more about this poem will find an interesting analysis in "Cummings in the Classroom" by Dolores Barracano Schmidt, from the February 1964 issue of *College Composition and Communication,* reprinted in James M. McCrimmon's *From Source to Statement* (Houghton Mifflin, 1968).

> "Who is this Hemingway,
> Who is this Proust?
>
> "Who is this Vladimir
> Whatchamacallit, this
> Neopostrealist
> Rabble?" she groused.

A poet might manage to be this amusing in a limerick or in couplets, but not in blank verse or the heroic quatrain. The double-dactyl lines ($\smile\smile/\smile\smile$) are a large part of the fun.

Besides using rhythmic stresses to help convey the poem's meaning, a poet can also produce sound effects through a careful choice and arrangement of his words. Many words have sounds that can be characterized as mellifluous or harsh, strong or gentle, crisp or lingering. "Pied Beauty" (p. 64) celebrates things that depart from classic regularity, that are interesting because of detail rather than form. The poem's trochee words, many involving *l* sounds that suggest "little"—*dappled, couple-colour, stipple, plotted, fallow, tackle, fickle, freckled*—help to give the effect of a small, repeated pattern. Pope, while using the heroic couplet as his basic form, has well illustrated the different sound effects that can be achieved from the selection and arrangement of words:

> Soft is the strain when Zephyr gently blows,
> And the smooth stream in smoother numbers flows;
> But when loud surges lash the sounding shore,
> The hoarse, rough verse should like the torrent roar;
> When Ajax strives some rock's vast weight to throw,
> The line too labors, and the words move slow;
> Not so, when swift Camilla scours the plain,
> Flies o'er the unbending corn, and skims along the main.

> —from *Essay on Criticism*, Part II

The sounds of *s, z, o,* and *oo* confer smoothness on the first

two lines. Rougher consonants and harsher vowel sounds characterize the third and fourth lines. Lines 5 and 6 are slowed up
with spondees (*Ajax, some rock's, vast weight, too lab,* and
move slow) instead of iambs, and Camilla's motion is made
more delicate by the extension of line 8 to include an extra foot,
and the portioning of the usual five stresses into six, each one
a little lighter.

Meaning can, then, be reinforced by the sounds of the words
that express it. When a word's sound actually imitates the
sound of what it stands for, it is an example of ONOMATOPOEIA.
Though not in large supply, such words can often be very effective in poetry—*babble, bang, boom, buzz, clang, click, cricket,
crunch, gong, honk, mew, pitter-patter, quack, whiz, zoom.* The
final line of Keats's "To Autumn," *And gathering swallows
twitter in the skies,* makes good use of *twitter,* whose pronunci-
ation sounds like the bird call it designates.

RHYTHM is the word used to describe orderly repetitions of
stress in poetry. There are several designations for repetitions
of sounds. ALLITERATION refers to the repetition of consonant
sounds that begin stressed syllables. *Fearful footfall,* for example, includes four syllables beginning with the sound of *f,*
but it is the *f*'s of the stressed *fear* and *foot* that, strictly, signify alliteration. (Sound, not spelling, is the criterion; *fearful
phantom* is also alliterative.) The syllables involved need not
be in contiguous words, but a reader's ear may forget the first
occurrence if alliterative consonants are separated by much
more than a line of poetry.

ASSONANCE means the repetition of stressed vowel sounds,
as in *beige lady.* In the passage from Pope quoted above,
Zephyr and *gently, loud* and *sounding, hoarse* and *roar* all cap-
italize upon the pleasure to the ear inherent in repeated stressed
vowel sounds. CONSONANCE refers to similar consonant sounds
following stressed vowel sounds, as in *make/like,* or, to turn
again to Pope's extract, *Ajax/rock's.*

Although rhyme has been discussed earlier, it may be useful to repeat a few of its principles. PERFECT RHYME or TRUE RHYME (as opposed to APPROXIMATE, HALF, NEAR, OFF, SLANT, IMPERFECT, or whatever name one wishes to give the more baroque music of rhyming sounds that do not meet all the requirements) describes a situation where the final stressed vowel sounds and everything following are identical. *Merrily* and *verily* are perfect rhymes, though *mineral* and *general* are not, except when made to rhyme through mispronunciation in a Gilbert and Sullivan operetta. Because three syllables are involved in the identity, *merrily* and *verily* are TRIPLE RHYMES; *double* and *trouble* are DOUBLE RHYMES or FEMININE RHYMES. SINGLE RHYME or MASCULINE RHYME (*tray/dismay*) are terms to describe a combination of assonance and consonance in a final syllable. When words that rhyme with each other fall at the ends of lines, they are called END RHYMES. INTERNAL RHYME is a term to designate the presence of rhyming sounds within a line, as in the first stanza of this seventeenth-century hymn:

> We gather together to ask the Lord's blessing,
> He chastens and hastens His will to make known;
> The wicked oppressing now cease them from distressing,
> Sing praises to His name, He forgets not His own.

Here *distressing* forms an end-rhyme pair with *blessing,* while *oppressing,* like *chastens* and *hastens,* is part of an internal-rhyme pattern.

A poet needs to listen closely to his own words to assure himself that he has chosen and arranged sounds so as to reinforce his meaning. Reading aloud should be part of his writing process for any poem intended to be heard.

There are memorable poems written for the ear that include no rhyme or other kinds of identical sounds. But, for many writers, achieving such pattern is a creative pleasure, and for

many listeners it is one of the delights of hearing poetry. One
prejudice that has produced some very bad poetry is the in-
sistence on rhyme as a poem's first principle. When word
choices are allowed to fumble, when arrangements are twisted
awkwardly, when meaning itself is pummeled and pushed into
a deformed shape in the interests of a rhyme pattern, the whole
poem becomes insipid, sometimes ridiculous. Rhyme is an interesting part of the poem only if it seems to enhance the idea
and the shape, only if it seems a functional part, inseparable
from the rest. Even when a rhyme pattern is a "given," as in a
sonnet, it should not look like a schedule of specifications that
requires the compromise of other values. It is better to avoid
rhyme altogether than to distort a poem, and some ideas find
better expression if rhyme is forgotten. Often, though, what a
rhyme-ridden poem really needs is not a complete jettisoning
of rhyme but better work on the pattern, more flexibility in the
use of slant rhymes, more revision and rearrangement of the
whole poem.

Sound repetitions should not be allowed to proliferate too
freely. A writer may consider himself lucky or clever to discover a whole string of sound repetitions with which to express
his idea, but for the reader too much of a good thing can become monotonous or just silly. When Shakespeare's Bottom the
Weaver (*A Midsummer Night's Dream*), in his role as Py-
ramus, speaks of the moon's *gracious, golden, glittering gleams*
and invites the Fates to *Quail, crush, conclude, and quell,* the
effect of so thorough an exploitation of similar sounds is hilari-
ous, as Shakespeare intended it to be. Robert Frost's "Design"
(p. 41) has already been described as an Italian sonnet with
an extra measure of rhyme. Seven of its fourteen lines end in
white or perfect rhymes for *white;* yet the rhyming does not
seem obtrusive. In an earlier version, however, Frost managed
to rhyme all six lines of the sestet with the result that ten of

the fourteen lines ended with *white* or its rhymes. This was a remarkable accomplishment, but Frost apparently felt he had gone too far, that he had pushed rhyming beyond its optimum point to a monotonous extreme.

A rhyming dictionary, though of less use than either a standard dictionary or a thesaurus, probably belongs on the reference shelf of the working poet. For serious poetry, such a book should be used cautiously, not as the prop on which the writing of a poem depends. The enthusiastic amateur who decides to write a sonnet, gets his schedule of rhyming words from a rhyming dictionary, then proceeds to "fill in the blanks" with other words cannot hope to achieve a poem that is tolerable. The most effective use of a rhyming dictionary usually comes after the poem is well underway. The hurdle of a line that won't fit into the rhyme pattern or the need for a rhyming partner for a good word already chosen may send the poet to his rhyming dictionary. Since English isn't rich in rhyming sounds, his chances of finding the right word are not large. He may make a useful discovery. But if he fails to find any workable suggestion either among the perfect rhymes or among any slant rhymes he can think of, he will at least know that he had better revise what he has already written, either to rearrange words or to reorganize his rhyme pattern.

For the light verse writer, however, the rhyming dictionary can be a more constant and rewarding companion. Most light verse involves rhyme, and the humor often depends on cleverness in rhyming, the surprise of unexpected pairs like Ogden Nash's *copy/jalopy, abhorrence/Florence, stripling/Kipling*. For this kind of poetry, the rhyming dictionary can be a point of departure, a rich source of suggestions for amusing lines. It is unlikely that a competent serious poem ever has its origin in a pair of rhyming words, but from such a beginning a writer may be able to devise a delightful piece of light verse.

JOURNAL PROJECTS

31. Consider the various meters and lengths of line that you have
    been reading about. Choose what you think would be the best
    metrical line for a poem about each of the following topics if
    you wished to use rhythm appropriately.
    a. A horse race.
    b. A waltz.
    c. The movement of a glacier.
    d. The autumn flight of mallards to the south.
32. Following the pattern of "Said" (p. 94), try to write your own
    double-dactyl poem.
33. For each of the following qualities, make a list of words whose
    sounds seem to suggest that quality:
    a. Harshness
    b. Heaviness
    c. Lack of harmony
    d. Softness (sound)
34. Look again at the sonnet you have been working on (Projects
    #12, #24, #30). Re-examine any inversions of normal order
    you have used. Are these necessary, justifiable, graceful? Can
    you make changes that would improve word order? Can you
    make changes that would result in a more effective use of sound?
35. Return to your persuasive poem in free verse (Projects #7, #16,
    #24, #30). Have you used rhythm or sound identities to en-
    hance meaning? If not, ought you introduce either or both?

ᘔ MAKING IMAGES

In poetry, an IMAGE is an expression that suggests or conveys a sensory impression to the reader or listener. Advising a poet to use imagery is rather like advising a baker to use flour. Although it is possible to write a poem with no imagery whatever, it isn't easy. Poems vary widely, however, in the degree to which they appeal to a reader's five senses. "A Kiss" (p. 51) uses very little imagery. Here is another poem in which imagery is of limited importance:

The Descent

The descent beckons
       as the ascent beckoned.
           Memory is a kind
of accomplishment,
       a sort of renewal
           even
an initiation, since the spaces it opens are new places
       inhabited by hordes
           heretofore unrealized,

of new kinds—
       since their movements
           are towards new objectives
(even though formerly they were abandoned).

NO DEFEAT is made up entirely of defeat—since
the world it opens is always a place
     formerly
        unsuspected. A
world lost,
   a world unsuspected,
      beckons to new places
and no whiteness (lost) is so white as the memory
of whiteness.

WITH EVENING, love wakens
   though its shadows
     which are alive by reason
of the sun shining—
   grow sleepy now and drop away
     from desire. . . .

LOVE WITHOUT shadows stirs now
   beginning to awaken
     as night
advances. . . .

THE DESCENT
   made up of despairs
     and without accomplishment
realizes a new awakening:
   which is a reversal
of despair.
   For what we cannot accomplish, what
is denied to love,
   what we have lost in the anticipation—
     a descent follows,
endless and indestructible. . . .

               —William Carlos Williams (1883–1963)

These lines are arranged to interest the eye, but most of the
words do not ask the reader to envision anything. Such statements as *Memory is a kind/of accomplishment* and *NO DE-*

FEAT is made up entirely of defeat use an abstract vocabulary that is addressed to the intellect rather than to the senses. A poet who uses the word *mountain* may depend upon it that each of his readers will imagine a picture; though no two of their pictures will be exactly the same, all will have a common mountainous element in them. A word like *accomplishment*, though, is not likely to suggest any picture. Those readers who do visualize something, e.g. reaching the top of a ladder or solving a chess puzzle, will see a private picture based on personal experience and not shared by others. A poet cannot use *accomplishment* to convey anything but a general impression, an idea. The verb *beckons*, though, does carry an image; most readers will probably, if only for a moment, "see" the gesture of beckoning, just as they will "see" white in the rather intellectualized comment about whiteness. The most sustained use of imagery, however, is contained in the two stanzas beginning *WITH EVENING*, where love's waking up at night and love's shadows growing sleepy and dropping away as the sun concedes to darkness invite the mind to visualize a changing scene. The scene is not entirely clear. (Does one, for example, see love incorporated in a human figure or figures?) But the change of light and shadow will probably register in the mind's eye.

The word "image" suggests a visual impression, but any or all of the senses can be involved in poetic imagery. Sight and sound are the most frequently used, but writers can also evoke impressions of taste and smell and, of course, touch, including sensations of texture, density, temperature, motion, pain, etc.

Poets use imagery for a variety of reasons. In some poems, the transfer of a sense experience from poet to reader is a major reason for the poem. May Swenson was intrigued with the sight of the Pigeon Woman among her birds and wanted the reader to see it, too. Her poem (p. 4) contains many images, most of them visual, some suggesting sound and touch, that taken all together make a larger image, a complete scene in which an action takes place. Some poems use imagery for its decorative effects, to produce local color or a special atmosphere. Keats's "The Eve of St. Agnes" is a narrative poem, its chief concern the story of a daring elopement. But the narrative strain is richly embroidered with details about the cold night, the castle, the appearance of the hero and heroine, the lady's boudoir, a midnight feast, and these enrich the romantic and medieval flavor.

It is important that a poet understand how an image is to operate in his poem. Is the image to be there for its own sake, a descriptive detail to be transferred to the reader, or has it a further function—to evoke a mood or train of thought, or to represent something that is not mentioned in the poem? Consider, for example, this poem of two triplet stanzas:

The Eagle

> He clasps the crag with crooked hands;
> Close to the sun in lonely lands,
> Ringed with the azure world, he stands.
>
> The wrinkled sea beneath him crawls;
> He watches from his mountain walls,
> And like a thunderbolt he falls.

> —Alfred, Lord Tennyson (1809–1892)

These lines describe an eagle so as to suggest a clear picture to the reader. And that is the purpose of the imagery, its only purpose. Rereading the two *haiku* on p. 67, one observes that each of these also encloses an image clear enough for the reader to envision. But one is nagged into supposing that the image is not the whole point, partly because the news has gotten out that there is always more than meets the eye in a *haiku*, partly because the description seems designed to evoke a mood and is open-ended rather than complete. The writer, his imagination captured by an observation, has put it into words in a way that will not only convey the picture but will also give rise to a train of thought. The empty, scratched pond in the moonlight is the image, but adhering to the picture are unstated suggestions of loneliness, the vestiges of human activity on the natural landscape, the sense of peace that pervades the natural world vacated of human inhabitants, the emptiness of winter. The image is transferred not only for its own sake but to trigger these musings.

A poet can invent an image that is the medium of exchange between his feelings and his reader's feelings. MacLeish has illustrated this technique in "Ars Poetica"—*For all the history of grief/An empty doorway and a maple leaf.* The writer experiences an emotion, grief. He chooses some image that seems to stand for that emotion. The reader receives the image, that is, he "sees" the picture, and, if it works effectively, he also senses the grief that the picture represents. The doorway and the maple leaf are, then, a kind of artistic coinage, concrete and abbreviated currency for the abstract and large feelings that grief includes. T. S. Eliot once called this kind of image an OBJECTIVE CORRELATIVE, something in the external world that the senses can apprehend that is the equivalent of an intangible mood or feeling.

The process of making poetic imagery is a selective one. The poet is not a camera photographing the whole scene or a tape recorder preserving all the sounds in an experience. If he is skillful, he chooses only those details that relate to the poem's purpose, and to the impression he wishes the reader to receive. Walt Whitman in "A Noiseless Patient Spider" (p. 39) provides no information about the size, shape, color, or texture of his spider, although he must have observed these particulars. Only the spider's motions are essential to the poem, and these are what he has included. Robert Frost, on the other hand, ignores motion in favor of the spider's whiteness, fatness, dimpled body, details that contribute to the theme of "Design" (p. 41).

All the discussion so far (though not all of the examples) has treated imagery as having literal meaning. Tennyson's verbal picture of an eagle describes a "real" eagle that is the poem's real subject. Parts of the total image, though, are not literal. An ornithologist would find it whimsically inaccurate to describe the bird's claws as *crooked hands*. A meteorologist might question the eagle's fall as being like a *thunderbolt;* furthermore, he would probably argue that thunder isn't a bolt, that this concept is a holdover from the mythical figure of Zeus hurling thunder at chosen targets. In both these instances, Tennyson has used images figuratively. So many poetic images are incorporated into various figures of speech that these will be separately considered in the next section.

JOURNAL PROJECTS

36. List as many words and phrases as you can think of to try to make each of these sense experiences vivid for a reader:
    a. A toothache
    b. The smell of apples being pressed into cider
    c. Touching velvet
    d. The noise of a plane breaking the sound barrier
    e. Tasting prepared mustard
    f. The sound of a freight train to someone standing nearby
    g. Looking at a waterfall
    h. Handling wet putty or clay

37. Return to Project #5, your descriptive poem about the execution. Have you used imagery? To what senses do the images appeal? Are you able to sharpen any of the images to make the poem more effective?

38. Look again at the four *haiku* you tried to write for Project #25. In each, does the image suggest a mood that will carry the reader beyond the poem into further contemplation?

USING FIGURATIVE LANGUAGE

Figurative language includes a variety of techniques for saying things that are not literally true, although they may be imaginatively and artistically convincing. The aim in figures of speech is not to deceive, since their distance from actual fact is much too evident to be deceptive. Their purpose, instead, is to make or suggest new and sometimes surprising relationships, to bring elements that are usually separate into combination.

Although the technical distinctions between one figure of speech and another are not the poet's most important concern, it is useful, at first, to understand the various types and to see how they work in poetry. To begin, then, a figurative AL-LUSION is a hint or mention of an event or person in history, legend, fiction, or current affairs that is outside the poem's literal sense but can be related to it. A poem that is openly about John the Baptist can scarcely be said to allude to his story; the poem partly tells the story. But when T. S. Eliot's J. Alfred Prufrock says *I have seen my head . . . brought in upon a platter,* he is alluding to the death of John. Such allusions are part of casual conversations as well as of literature: a demanding boss is labeled Simon Legree; owners of vacation cottages have been known to name them Shangri-La. Such references assume that the listener or reader will quickly comprehend a complex of implications that each allusion suggests, qualities spelled out in detail in the original history or story.

The use of allusions poses serious problems for a poet. If he counts upon his readers' receiving a certain idea, he must be certain that his allusion is to something generally known. Readers vary considerably in what they know, but it is usually safe to assume that most are somewhat familiar with the Bible, Greek and Roman mythology, the important events in the history of Europe and North America, widely read plays, poems, and prose in English, and widely circulated aphorisms, movies, and news stories. One is justified in expecting his reader to "get" allusions to Noah, the Trojan Horse, Charlemagne, Macbeth, Frankenstein, the Mad Hatter, Custer's Last Stand, the New Deal, Greta Garbo, the Beatles, and other persons, items, and events, both fictional and real, that are familiar to the English-speaking public. But the more surely known the object of allusion, the more probable that it has been alluded to in earlier work, with the result that it may be stale. Readers are tired of Pyrrhic victories and Waterloos, Galahads and Horatio Algers. No allusion at all would be better than one so shopworn.

Perhaps a working poet should avoid all very familiar allusions and, when using those that are not certain to be recognized, make it a rule never to let the whole poem depend on the allusion. Archibald MacLeish has written a poem about the relentless passage of time called "You, Andrew Marvell." That reader who knows Marvell's poem about time, "To His Coy Mistress," is better prepared to enjoy the later poem that alludes to it; on the other hand, MacLeish's poem is sufficiently self-contained to convey its idea even to the reader for whom the allusion remains a mystery. But the incidental allusion can sometimes cause trouble. An undergraduate term paper, for example, undertook to analyze Wallace Stevens's "Peter Quince at the Clavier." The poem does not depend on the reader's being able to identify Peter Quince (a clown in *A Midsummer Night's Dream*), though this would be extra, helpful knowledge. The paper, however, was based on the careless assumption that the allusion was to Peter Quint, an evil, ghostly valet in Henry James's *The Turn of the Screw*. It was remarkable how logical an analysis was developed according to this faulty assumption, an object lesson about the dangers of the obscure allusion and about too-hasty identification by the reader. When used well, though, an allusion can be valuable in suggesting to the reader, through a word or two, a complete motif stored in his repertoire of information.

PERSONIFICATION is a figure of speech in which something that is not human is given human qualities. When Tennyson refers to the eagle's *crooked hands,* he is for the moment asking the reader to imagine that the bird has hands like an old man's. The clock in "Eight O'Clock" (p. 12) is given the volition to collect its strength and strike, much as though it were a conscious and deliberate person. These are rather fleeting allusions to humanness. The term PATHETIC FALLACY, invented by John Ruskin, describes a particular variety of personification— the fallacy, or, more accurately, the poetic license of ascribing capacities for feeling to inanimate objects. In older poems, one often encounters examples of abstractions described in detail as complete persons. Emily Dickinson's "Soul" (p. 28) is developed in this way. Possibly because of an overuse of such figures as Mother Nature and Father Time, this kind of figure is not popular with contemporary poets. The gentleman in a dustcoat in John Crowe Ransom's "Piazza Piece" (p. 6), probably a personification of death, is rather exceptional. Personification, whether completely developed or merely hinted, can have the effect of simultaneously conferring concreteness and animation on the abstract and inanimate. There is a general tendency to project human qualities upon the world at large, and personification expresses this tendency.

The last line of Tennyson's "The Eagle" reads *And like a thunderbolt he falls.* The reader is asked to entertain a comparison between a thunderbolt and an eagle, and this specified comparison is called a SIMILE. Words such as *like, as, so,* and comparative modifiers with *than* are the usual signals of a simile, provided that the two things being compared are dissimilar. To say that parasols are like umbrellas is explanation preliminary to a full definition. But to say that parasols are like flowers unfolding on a sunny day is to create a simile, though not a very good one. Robert Burns's *O My Luve's like a red, red rose* asks the reader not to believe that the girl and the rose are identical but that they share some elements in common. These common qualities are not named, but they might include beauty, freshness, softness, smoothness, fragrance, and perhaps the poignant inevitability of early fading.

One paradox of figurative language is that metaphors are more patently untrue than similes, but often they are more spontaneously made and more easily accepted. A METAPHOR does not use *as* or an equivalent signal to announce its comparison but either openly or subtly fuses two dissimilar things. *All the world's a stage* boldly proposes that the world is like the locus for a theatrical performance, and the reader assents, seeing various similarities—mankind playing roles, the brevity of the performance, perhaps a director and script behind the scenes to control events.

Two lines from Yeats's "Sailing to Byzantium" demonstrate the force of a good metaphor:

> An aged man is but a paltry thing,
> A tattered coat upon a stick . . .

The first predicate nominative in this sentence, *but a paltry thing,* is not figurative but literal. And the words seem to have been selected to prevent any image at all: *thing* is vague and shapeless; one knows more or less what *paltry* means, but the word's origins are obscure. Then comes the metaphoric image, *A tattered coat upon a stick,* asking the reader to accept the similarity between an old man and a scarecrow. The fusion between these two seems so "right" that the reader will probably assent without thinking. If he does try to discover points of similarity, he will find several. An old man's flesh is likely to have shriveled, leaving his bones as prominent as the frame for a scarecrow, something that does not fill but holds up clothes. An old man and his clothes often seem worn out, shabby, and so does the scarecrow. The scarecrow in the field is put there to frighten birds and to protect corn; it is a grotesque intrusion into the natural processes. So an old man, a kind of *memento mori* to the young, is outside the natural activities of love and procreation, growth and mobility.

When *a* is said to be *b*, the metaphor makes an open statement of similarity. There are, though, many opportunities to submerge the metaphor in such a way that it slides into the reader's mind almost unnoticed. *The winter of our discontent, my heart leaps up, a glancing blow* all subtly incorporate metaphors. Similes and metaphors offer the poet opportunities to express unique comparisons and to make abstractions concrete, but they are different in the way they operate in a poem and in how they are received by the reader. A simile, in making its comparison explicit, keeps somewhat separate items that are fused in a metaphor. The reader of a metaphor is likely to discover that he has effortlessly absorbed the idea that two things are similar. When he encounters a simile, he will probably be conscious of the intellectual process of comparison.

The meaning of a metaphor is quite different from the literal meaning of its image. No one hearing Macbeth talk of *life's fitful fever* is likely to suppose that he means influenza or any other actual fever; the mind deftly translates *fitful fever* into something like "the intermittent stresses and anxieties of human life." An image that is a SYMBOL, on the other hand, means what it says, although it means other things too. The symbol of the cross, for example, exactly represents the cross of the

crucifixion; but it may also mean Jesus, or the philosophy of
Christianity, or the Christian Church, or the idea of martyr-
dom, and in some cases all of these together. The poet who
uses a symbolic image expects that image to be received literally, but he also hopes that it will radiate certain overtones
to give his reader a rich response to a simple word or phrase.

In the world of events, certain symbols have so often been
used to carry these extra meanings that they are said to be conventional symbols. The flag, a wedding ring, the combination of cherry tree and hatchet—each of these quickly conveys
roughly the same meaning to everyone who participates in the
culture that generated them. (The cherry tree and hatchet
would be received only literally and without symbolic overtones by someone not immersed in this culture.) Sometimes
poets make good use of the efficient information-bearing capacities of conventional symbols, as in this case:

To the Snake

Green Snake, when I hung you round my neck
and stroked your cold, pulsing throat
        as you hissed to me, glinting
arrowy gold scales, and I felt
        the weight of you on my shoulders,
and the whispering silver of your dryness
        sounded close at my ears—

Green Snake—I swore to my companions that certainly
        you were harmless! But truly
I had no certainty, and no hope, only desiring
        to hold you, for that joy,
                                which left
a long wake of pleasure, as the leaves moved
and you faded into the pattern
of grass and shadows, and I returned
smiling and haunted, to a dark morning.

                              —Denise Levertov (1923–   )

One can get some enjoyment from this poem if the snake is considered to be merely a real snake. But the author has relied on its being recognized as a symbol established in Genesis, a symbol synthesizing glamour, evil, and knowledge that carries with it the threat of irreversible change. She expects her reader to remember the fall of man and to bring to this poem certain concepts about that event. With these concepts, he regards the lady as a latter-day Eve participating in an action that may involve dangers. Denise Levertov also relies on the conventional symbolism of the snake which Freud has established. The snake is phallic, and this poem strongly suggests a sexual episode.

(There are, of course, also metaphors and similes that have become conventional. The identification of life with a journey is one such. Or a life's span can be compared with a day in which youth = morning, maturity = afternoon, old age = evening or sunset, death = night; or with the seasons of the year in which youth = spring, etc.)

Other symbols, too original to be called conventional, seem so easy to understand and accept that they are referred to as NATURAL SYMBOLS. Robert Frost's image of choosing between two roads diverging in the wood, an image that also represents a decision point in life, is a good example.

A poet runs his greatest risks of not being understood or of being misunderstood when he invents a UNIQUE SYMBOL, one that has neither a background of habit nor natural appropriateness to help his reader. The following poem depends upon a single unique symbol:

Mushrooms

Overnight, very
Whitely, discreetly,
Very quietly

Our toes, our noses
Take hold on the loam,
Acquire the air.

Nobody sees us,
Stops us, betrays us;
The small grains make room.

Soft fists insist on
Heaving the needles,
The leafy bedding,

Even the paving.
Our hammers, our rams,
Earless and eyeless,

Perfectly voiceless,
Widen the crannies,
Shoulder through holes. We

Diet on water,
On crumbs of shadow,
Bland-mannered, asking

Little or nothing.
So many of us!
So many of us!

We are shelves, we are
Tables, we are meek,
We are edible,

Nudgers and shovers
In spite of ourselves.
Our kind multiplies:

We shall by morning
Inherit the earth.
Our foot's in the door.

—Sylvia Plath (1932–1963)

Here the mushrooms speak, giving the details of their growth and development. This poem is enjoyable at a literal level, as a poem about mushrooms who personify themselves in an imaginary chorus. The way they talk, though, and their veiled threats suggest that they may represent something more formidable than mushrooms. The many expressions of personification accumulate strangeness and urge the reader to think beyond the limits of botany, to wonder what these mushrooms might be. Are they encroaching "fungi" within a personality, or another species that will eventually predominate, or the earth's meek and lowly people, or people of another race, or secret visitors from another planet, or an avalanche of babies threatening to overrun the world? One cannot decide, but any or all of these would be interesting possibilities.

How does the poet using a symbol signal to his reader that more than literal meaning is intended? "Mushrooms" does this through the curious threats of the mushrooms; the hint of mystery in what they say suggests a further meaning. In other poems, notably Frost's two roads, a suggestion of symbol can be achieved by keeping the literal description quite spare. Too much specificity would fix the roads in the natural landscape too firmly. The use of just a few descriptive details makes the picture vaguer. And the last line, *And that has made all the difference,* confirms the reader's suspicion that the poem involves more than diverging roads.

Few contemporary poets seem interested in using ALLEGORY, although John Crowe Ransom has successfully incorporated this figure into "Captain Carpenter." An allegorical poem is a narrative poem in which each character and each episode stands for something else. One might call it an extended metaphor that encompasses events. The most famous allegory in English is in prose—*A Pilgrim's Progress.* Edward Taylor (see p. 36) has used the spider/wasp/fly episode as an allegory for man's struggle against the devil. Perhaps modern allegories are scarce because they are difficult to construct. To devise a plot and characters that exactly correspond to elements in the other, "real" situation requires considerable ingenuity, and the finished work always has a certain artificiality because the structure is so prominent.

These are, in brief, some of the technical differences that separate one figure of speech from another. They are useful for students who analyze what is already written in an effort to understand and appreciate poetry. For the writer of poetry too much concentration on these differences may overshadow the quality that figures of speech have in common—all present at least two elements (an abstraction and an image, or two images) and invite the reader to make imaginative connections between them, to notice their similarities.

The poet has decisions to make about figurative language that are more important than the choice between, say, a simile and a metaphor. Some of these decisions concern the place and function of the figure in the poem. Is the figure introduced sharply and briefly to accent a particular point, or does it pervade the whole poem and become the central interest? In the second stanza of Maxine Kumin's "Lately, at Night" (p. 59), the speaker says her dead father's profile is *like a cutaway/ springing erect in a child's pop-out book*. This simile conveys a clear picture of rigidity and of a visual paradox in which three dimensions seem to reduce to two. Having made this descriptive point, the image stops. Nothing else in the poem is quite like it or even hints at a return to the pop-out book. The poem that follows, on the other hand, uses one extended metaphor in such a way that the poem's whole point depends on the poetic equation, man = stalagmite:

A Civil Servant

While in this cavernous place employed
Not once was I aware

Of my officious other-self
  Poised high above me there,

My self reversed, my rage-less part,
  A slimy yellowish cone—
Drip, drip; drip, drip—so down the years
  I stalagmized in stone.

Now pilgrims to the cave, who come
  To chip off what they can,
Prod me with child-like merriment:
  "Look, look! It's like a man!"

                              —Robert Graves (1895–   )

The theme of this poem would probably read: constant suppression of one's natural feelings ultimately leads to a loss of humanity. That theme is made concrete and forceful through one detailed metaphor. The demonstration, fantastic though it is, becomes much more frightening than an abstract statement.

"A Noiseless Patient Spider" (p. 39) uses figurative language in another way. Linking the two halves of the poem, an extended simile in which the soul is compared to the spider, is a network of images about the sea, the seacoast, and boats. These images metaphorically describe activities of both the spider and the soul and make the connection between them stronger.

A figure that does not pervade the whole poem can be used alone or in association with others as part of a figurative network. The *crooked hands* of Tennyson's eagle are independent, unattached to any other image in the poem. Yeats's *tattered coat upon a stick* may look unattached at first, but a careful reading of the whole poem reveals that the metaphor exists in a matrix of related figures:

Sailing to Byzantium

I

That is no country for old men. The young
In one another's arms, birds in the trees

—Those dying generations—at their song,
The salmon-falls, the mackerel-crowded seas,
Fish, flesh, or fowl, commend all summer long
Whatever is begotten, born, and dies.
Caught in that sensual music all neglect
Monuments of unaging intellect.

2

An aged man is but a paltry thing,
A tattered coat upon a stick, unless
Soul clap its hands and sing, and louder sing
For every tatter in its mortal dress,
Nor is there singing school but studying
Monuments of its own magnificence;
And therefore I have sailed the seas and come
To the holy city of Byzantium.

3

O sages standing in God's holy fire
As in the gold mosaic of a wall,
Come from the holy fire, perne in a gyre,
And be the singing-masters of my soul.
Consume my heart away; sick with desire
And fastened to a dying animal
It knows not what it is; and gather me
Into the artifice of eternity.

4

Once out of nature I shall never take
My bodily form from any natural thing,
But such a form as Grecian goldsmiths make
Of hammered gold and gold enameling
To keep a drowsy Emperor awake,
Or set upon a golden bough to sing
To lords and ladies of Byzantium
Of what is past, or passing, or to come.

—William Butler Yeats (1865–1939)

The scarecrow is clearly indicated only once. But it seems to connect with references to birds, both real and artificial, to old-ness, tatters, summer, and, particularly, to the several comments about what is man-made rather than natural. The poem's metaphoric sailing encloses families of images that crisscross and interconnect so that no single figure in the poem is entirely separate from others.

Figures of speech typically have a concreteness that appeals to one or more of the senses. It is for the poet to decide whether his figure will go beyond the sense impression into the area of intellectual speculation. The dead profile as cutaway in a pop-out book suggests a picture to the reader, but goes no farther. It would be unfortunate if the reader were to muse about extensive areas of similarity. A pop-out book is something that is fun for children, the snap with which the cutaway jumps up, a surprise to evoke laughter and delight. A corpse in a coffin is not fun and not delightful. So this descriptive figure is best appreciated only at the sensory level. Yeats's scarecrow also makes its first appeal to the visual sense, but it can be subjected to a more cerebral examination without harm to the poem. Readers who grasp the similarity between old man and scarecrow because of their stance outside nature will be using their minds rather than their capacities to visualize, and the poem will be enriched by this philosophic speculation.

The poet who uses a figure of speech must also decide about whether he wants the figure to be firm and clear or clouded in some mystery. He will choose to "pin down" the meaning or to allow it some looseness, according to the impression he wants to create. The metaphor in "A Civil Servant" (p. 116) is unique and extremely complicated. A reader must keep in mind the separate pieces of the picture and think about the process of petrifaction. But it would be difficult to entertain any other meaning except the one clearly intended. With Robert Frost's simile, *a flower like froth* ("Design," p. 41), meaning is less

certain. What kind of froth is one to visualize? Sea foam?
Tulle? The froth on a glass of beer? The saliva of a mad dog?
One can establish a general idea but not the precise meaning.
In Sylvia Plath's poem, "Mushrooms" (p. 113), the meaning is
even more questionable, so mysteriously veiled that no one can
ever be sure he understands the significance of the mushrooms.
In each case, the degree of clarity has been deliberately chosen,
and, if there is mystery, it is no accident.

Besides the place that a figure of speech occupies in his poem,
the poet will also wish to consider its quality. When he makes
a new metaphor or simile or symbol, the poet is an inventor,
and it is part of his responsibility to test the viability of the invention. Imagine, to construct a simplistic example, a poet
seeking a metaphor for a tall, majestic woman. In the course
of his musings, he hits upon the idea of referring to her as an
obelisk. Whether this thought comes as a flash of inspiration or
whether he has hunted for it, he ought next to examine the
choice very carefully. Is there enough similarity between his
woman and his obelisk to win the reader's assent? Both are
towering, tall, and thin, imposing figures on their landscapes,
with clearly defined silhouettes. So far, so good. But is this
enough resemblance to make the metaphor work? Probably
not. The reader feels uneasy, as though tallness alone, and
vastly different degrees of tallness at that, has been used to
force the comparison upon him. There are disturbing differences between woman and obelisk that are almost certain to
overwhelm the similarities. The obelisk is especially inanimate;
it has straight sides that seem to resist connection with a human
form; it is stone; it has square edges; it comes to a sharp point
at the top. The obelisk's shape is, in fact, so definite and so
indelible in the mind's eye that it upsets the metaphor. The
poet would do better with a vaguer word like "tower," or one
that already has human qualities built in, like "statue," or one

that emphasizes majesty as well as height, like "Athena." Robert Frost once used a silken tent in a simile to describe a gracefully majestic woman; even without knowing the whole poem, one can sense that this is more convincing than the obelisk.

The poet working with figures of speech has two opposite troubles to avoid—the over-familiar figure on the one hand and, on the other, the figure so private and original as to be baffling or altogether obscure. Those figures that are too familiar include not only stale, trite expressions from common speech (*dead as a doornail, beyond the pale, the horns of a dilemma,* etc.) but also figures whose use has been memorably appropriated by another poet. Since Yeats has already done so, who can now compare an old man and a scarecrow? If the image of a scarecrow is to enter a poem, it had best be introduced literally or in a figure very different in meaning from Yeats's. Does a poet, then, accidentally acquire the monopoly on a figure, even sometimes on an image, by incorporating it into his poem? Frustrating though it may be for other writers, the answer is "yes," provided his poem is good enough to be widely read. It is some comfort to realize that there must still be thousands of arresting comparisons that have not yet been used in eminent poems.

The figure that is too exclusive is usually the product of some personal association of ideas so peculiar to the poet himself that it cannot gain a reader's assent. A poet may have good reason in his own history or psychology to see sunrise as a symbol of illness or to speak of love metaphorically as a fish, but he will have to be very skillful to make such strange figures work in his poetry. Though it is difficult to make the similarities in some combinations clear and forceful, it is always worth trying if the poet himself is confident about the relationship. A poet runs special risks when he takes an image that is part of a conventional or natural figure (or, to put it another way, has certain established or obvious connotations) and uses it in a different way. This can be achieved, though, if the writer's hand is sure. Most people would probably agree that the image of a hawk carries with it ideas of preying, of swooping and violent attacks, of strength without pity. That the hawk has these established connotations has recently been demonstrated; the "hawk/dove" dichotomy vis-à-vis foreign policy already seemed a cliché when it was first enunciated. Yet Thoreau, in the section of *Walden* called "Spring," uses the hawk very differently. Its spiraling, gliding flight is described in such a way that the hawk seems to symbolize the aspirations and renewals of spring and of the human spirit in spring. It is a bold stroke, but it works well. This should be encouraging proof to a new poet that even a daringly original figure can succeed if it has innate appropriateness not previously discovered and if it is skillfuly placed in the whole work.

Journal Projects

39. Think of an appropriate allusion from history, fiction, or current affairs that is neither trite nor esoteric for each of these abstractions:
    a. Indecision
    b. Courage against great odds
    c. Illusions of grandeur
    d. Opulence
    e. Treason
    f. Stinginess
    g. Misanthropy
    h. Perseverance

40. Write a series of small metaphors for death, deciding for each whether it is conventional, natural, or unique. Could those that are unique be made meaningful for a reader if they were incorporated into poems?

41. Using any form and any subject, construct a short poem that tries to explain some abstraction through a series of metaphors and/or similes.

42. Using any form and any subject, construct a short poem whose theme is dependent upon one extended metaphor or simile.

SAYING THINGS IN CIRCUITOUS WAYS

There are other non-literal ways of saying things that are sometimes lumped together with metaphors and similes as figures of speech. These include puns, hyperbole (overstatement), understatement, paradox, oxymoron, and verbal irony. Insofar as they are not literally true and that each such device involves the reader in seeing at least two things in combination, they are indeed figures of speech. But in other respects they are different from the figures already treated.

For one thing, the comparison suggested in each of these verbal devices is more likely to ask the reader to contemplate differences rather than similarities. When Macbeth says metaphorically that *Life's but a walking shadow,* etc., the reader probably sees both similarities and differences between life and the shadow, but the similarities dominate. When Marc Antony, though, ironically proclaims *For Brutus is an honorable man,* the audience focuses on the difference between *Brutus* and *honorable man* and suspects that Brutus has not been entirely honorable in murdering Caesar.

Secondly, the associations made in these figures rest more in the language itself than in the ideas behind the words. Most metaphors and similes can be translated into another tongue and retain their meaning. One gets into trouble, though, in attempting to translate puns or paradoxes or ironical statements because so much of the meaning depends on the way the language itself is organized and on the cultural matrix in which it works. Furthermore, these verbal devices are in general more sophisticated than most metaphors and similes, which ordinarily appeal to the senses. Even those readers who refrain from abstract thought or sustained cerebration of any kind can enjoy expressions like *A slumber did my spirit seal* or *the flints of love;* but it requires an act of the intellect to appreciate Hamlet's *A little more than kin and less than kind.*

At its silliest level, the PUN (two meanings for one sound) forms the backbone of children's jokes and riddles (e.g. *What's black and white and red all over?* where the point rests in a confusion between *red* and *read*). But the pun can be enriching as well as exasperating, serious as well as playful. In the line from *Hamlet* quoted above, *kind* is a pun. For the Elizabethan audience, the word meant both "natural" and, as in our most frequent use, "considerate" or "gentle in behavior." Hamlet is sardonically commenting that his uncle who is also his stepfather is (a) not a natural type of relation and (b) not considerate. Robert Frost's "Design" (p. 41) contains a pun in the line, *Mixed ready to begin the morning right.* References to witchcraft and mystery in the poem alert the reader's mind to the dual possibilities of *right* and *rite,* and both are appropriate in the poem. Good puns are hard to make and, since some people seem to have a special gift for punning, it is probably not wise for the ungifted to try too hard. The pun that works well in a poem enables the poet to amaze or amuse his reader by calling attention to the wide gap between two different meanings, both somehow appropriate, for the same sound or for two sounds that are almost the same.

The poet who uses HYPERBOLE, or overstatement, invites his reader to consider the gap between the probable truth and its exaggerated verbal expression. As in all figures of speech, the intention is not to deceive but to emphasize an impression. In early love poems, for example, the poet who claimed to be dying of a broken heart that could be mended only by a word or smile from his beloved did not expect his lady or his reader to believe him, but he did expect them to recognize how intense the affection must be to stimulate so excessive a claim. When the poet seems wryly aware of his own exaggeration and therefore is somewhat removed from emotional involvement, the effect is humorous, as in this love poem:

> Out upon it! I have loved
> > Three whole days together;
> And am like to love three more,
> > If it prove fair weather.
>
> Time shall molt away his wings,
> > Ere he shall discover
> In the whole wide world again
> > Such a constant lover.
>
> But the spite on 't is, no praise
> > Is due at all to me:
> Love with me had made no stays
> > Had it any been but she.
>
> Had it any been but she,
> > And that very face,
> There had been at least ere this
> > A dozen dozen in her place.
>
> > > —Sir John Suckling (1609–1642)

These lines contain several overstatements. The speaker pretends to be astonished at himself for being in love such a long time, that is, three days. He pretends that this is a record, not only for him, but for the whole world in every age. Only one exceptional lady could have inspired this magnificent fidelity, he continues, otherwise he would, in the past three days, have been in love with a *dozen dozen* others, a count that might stagger even Don Juan.

UNDERSTATEMENT seems to be more comfortable than overstatement for many contemporary poets. Here again, the reader is asked to contemplate a gap between fact and its verbal expression, but in understatement the verbal expression is paler, less explicit, less complete than the reality seems to require. The effect is one of sophisticated restraint, a kind of coolness. Andrew Marvell's "To His Coy Mistress" contains a famous example. A lover, begging his lady not to waste time with coyness, reminds her that life is short and the time left for love very limited:

> The grave's a fine and private place,
> But none, I think, do there embrace.

What the speaker would say if he were accurate is that, in the grave, one can do nothing at all, that all sense, breath, motion, feeling are over. But instead of delineating this nothingness, he mentions only that people don't make love when they are dead, and he accents the understatement by interjecting *I think,* as though he were venturing an opinion instead of cold fact.

A PARADOX is an apparent contradiction that can be resolved. The reader sees both an impossibility and its solution by sensing two meanings for the same expression. One of Emily Dickinson's poems begins with the statement, *My life closed twice before its close.* If the reader confines himself to a single meaning for *close,* the line makes no sense; one cannot die twice before he dies. To appreciate the paradox, he will have to recognize that the first two closings do not refer to physical death but to a cataclysmic numbing of the spirit that is like the end of life but is not actually the end. The poet who uses paradox is addressing himself to the reader's mind rather than to his senses or feelings. One has to figure out how to resolve an apparent contradiction, and this is usually a cerebral process.

An OXYMORON is a short, tight paradox, a statement of opposites that the reader can accept as credible. The song title, "The Sounds of Silence," is a good example. When E. E. Cummings says that his father *moved through dooms of love* and *depths of height* and *griefs of joy,* he brings opposites together in a way that makes sense. One can see clearly that the resolution of an oxymoron's contradiction is quicker, more spontaneous, and less reasoned than the resolution of a paradox. There is something that seems immediately convincing about *depths of height,* and the reader can accept it without puzzling out the meaning. For the poet, oxymoron offers a compact means for encompassing opposites, for collapsing a whole spectrum of states or degrees into a crisp and original expression.

VERBAL IRONY is the device of saying one thing and meaning something very different. Both understatement and overstatement are forms of verbal irony, but the term is more often applied to situations where a speaker means the exact opposite of what he says. "I have bad news for you—your horse won the Kentucky Derby!" really means "I have *good* news for you," and follows the basic ironic pattern. When Shakespeare in a song about winter describes the owl's call *To-whit tu-who!* as *a merry note,* he is being ironic. The owl's call is eerie, or chilling, or sad, or lonely, or mournful, but all its qualities are the opposites of merry. Here is a poem that makes extensive use of verbal irony:

Coup de Grâce

> Just at that moment the Wolf,
> Shag jaws and slavering grin,
> Steps from the property wood.
> O, what a gorge, what a gulf

Opens to gobble her in,
Little Red Riding Hood!

O, what a face full of fangs!
Eyes like saucers at least
Roll to seduce and beguile.
Miss, with her dimples and bangs,
Thinks him a handsome beast;
Flashes the Riding Hood Smile;

Stands her ground like a queen,
Velvet red of the rose
Framing each little milk-tooth,
Pink tongue peeping between.
Then, wider than anyone knows,
Opens her minikin mouth

Swallows up Wolf in a trice;
Tail going down gives a flick,
Caught as she closes her jaws.
Bows, all sugar and spice,
O, what a lady-like trick!
O, what a round of applause!

—A. D. Hope (1907–   )

This reversal of a familiar story, presented as a small theatrical episode, culminates in the poet's comment, *O, what a lady-like trick!* Since Red Riding Hood has ruthlessly and without warning ingested the wolf, one assumes either that *lady-like* is used ironically (i.e. Red Riding Hood is *not* lady-like) or that the author means what he says (i.e. this is the way ladies act) and is calling attention to an irony in the usual meaning of *lady-like*. In any case, while seeming to praise, he is obviously adversely disposed to Red Riding Hood, and he empathizes with the wolf. The *dimples, bangs, milk-tooth, pink tongue,* and *miniken mouth,* which, at first reading, may suggest innocence and softness, seem, in the light of the poem's ending, to be ironic descriptions for what is simpering and unpleasant.

The poet who uses irony, either in bitterness or for fun, must try to avoid the risk of being taken literally, of having the reader get the opposite of the intended meaning. A. D. Hope has signaled his irony by having Red Riding Hood close her *jaws* (rather than *mouth* or *lips*) before she bows, *all sugar and spice,* a clue to the carnivorous action under the saccharine pretense. The word *lady-like* is a surer indication, and the exclamation marks following the last two lines exaggerate approval to the point where it seems questionable.

Although they are not verbal devices, it may be useful to mention two other kinds of irony that offer interesting opportunities to writers of poetry. DRAMATIC IRONY describes a situation where the reader sees more and knows more than the speaker in a poem and where the speaker unwittingly involves himself in self-relevation that he doesn't intend. In some poems, the speaker is accepted as knowledgeable and as an accurate interpreter of himself and his situation; these are in no sense ironic. The reader is given no reason to doubt Sylvia Plath's mushrooms (p. 113); he believes them when they say they are numerous and that they will inherit the earth. But he doesn't believe the lady in Ransom's "Piazza Piece" (p. 6). She thinks she is waiting for a lover and objects that an old man is hovering nearby. The reader, though, suspects that the old man is Death, and that he is the surprise lover who will claim his lady soon.

IRONY OF SITUATION describes an inappropriateness in circumstances, a gap between what might logically be expected and the sad or funny or grotesque reality. Here is a poem in which an ironic situation is presented in such a way as to evoke the reader's criticism, perhaps even his determination to seek reform:

The Golf Links

The golf links lie so near the mill
   That almost every day
The laboring children can look out
   And see the men at play.

—Sarah N. Cleghorn (1876–1959)

Children working while men play is the opposite of what seems fitting and proper, just as Richard Cory's suicide (p. 78) is the opposite of what one might predict for a fortunate person. Both poems unfold ironic situations.

The last five sections have discussed several processes that the writing of poems involves—choosing words, arranging words, making images, using figurative language, saying things in circuitous ways—some of them difficult and technical. Perhaps the beginning poet will understand these more clearly after examining a poem that successfully makes use of these processes:

Deciduous Branch

Winter, that coils in the thickets now,
Will glide from the fields; the swinging rain
Be knotted with flowers; on every bough
A bird will meditate again.

Lord, in the night if I should die,
Who entertained your thrilling worm,
Corruption wastes more than the eye
Can pick from this imperfect form.

I lie awake, hearing the drip
Upon my sill; thinking, the sun
Has not been promised; we who strip
Summer to seed shall be undone.

Now, while the antler of the eaves
Liquefies, drop by drop, I brood

On a Christian thing: unless the leaves
Perish, the tree is not renewed.

If all our perishable stuff
Be nourished to its rot, we clean
Our trunk of death, and in our tough
And final growth are evergreen.

                                        —Stanley Kunitz (1905–   )

For this poem that looks forward from winter to spring, Stanley Kunitz has chosen a vocabulary that falls somewhere between formal and colloquial. Perhaps five words are especially arresting because they seem unusual choices, original to the point where they surprise—*swinging* (line 2), *entertained* and *thrilling* (line 6), *antler* (line 13), and *thing* (line 15).

One might expect rain to be blown or to slant; *swinging* introduces the image of ropes or chains that can be decorated with flowers, perhaps for a maypole dance. Stanley Kunitz apparently chose *swinging* to make pleasant sense impressions involving sight and motion. The definition of *thrilling* that comes first to mind is probably "causing intense emotion," and this fits the poem well. But the word also means "vibrating" or "causing vibration," qualities that suggest the worm in its bare physical sense. Some readers may remember an older meaning —"boring, piercing, penetrating," very appropriate for an actual worm, and very appropriate, too, in connection with *entertain,* for which meanings like "hold," "maintain," "keep in one's service" are older than the two current favorites, "to amuse" or "to receive as a guest."

Antler has a clear denotation and immediately conveys to the reader the picture of a deer's antler. The *antler of the eaves* is another way of saying "icicle," chosen because of similarities in their two shapes, but, of more importance, because antlers, like the leaves of a deciduous tree, fall in season. The *antler* metaphor links the branch and the icicle and, by extension, the seasons. *Christian thing,* though it sounds vague, is a precise choice of words. The author is talking about a Christian idea of life achieved only through death, the path through perishing to renewal. Why not say *Christian philosophy,* or *tenet,* or *creed,* or *doctrine,* all more specific than *thing?* The vagueness, though, carries information about the speaker in the poem. He is not a religious man quoting chapter and verse about a subject that is his central concern; he is, instead, a secular man with secular thoughts, reminded incidentally of something he holds as background information, the Christian paradox of life in death. Each of the poem's peculiar words turns out to be a purposeful and effective choice. Perhaps such choices came easily, but they may have taken months, even years.

The poem is rather unexceptional in respect to the arrangement of words. Kunitz has considered both sight and sound, with perhaps somewhat more attention to sound. The stanza pattern, tetrameter quatrains with the iamb as dominant foot and with the rhyme scheme *abab,* seems appropriate, but one is not overwhelmed by its special appropriateness; other forms might have done as well. Syntactically, the poem is fairly conventional. The few irregularities—the inversion in *Lord, in the night if I should die,* the omission of *will* before *Be knotted,* and the statement *Corruption wastes* instead of the expected *Corruption will waste*—are justifiable changes in normal syntax to fit the form, and the fact that they may have been maneuvered to fit the form is not obvious enough to rob the poem of grace.

The lines make extensive use of imagery. A few of the images have value because of the literal sense impressions they convey (*fields, flowers, bird, drip, sill*), but most are incorporated into figures of speech of various kinds. The allusion implicit in *a Christian thing* has already been mentioned; it is one of a family of religious allusions. The reader who recognizes that *Lord, in the night if I should die* resembles the line from a children's prayer, *If I should die before I wake,* will have a richer experience in reading the poem. It is useful, too, if *thrilling worm* reminds the reader of the serpent of Eden, the devil; if *the sun/Has not been promised* reminds him of God's covenant with Noah; and if *liquefy* reminds him of various medieval miracles about the liquefying blood of dead martyrs.

Personification is not an important element in "Deciduous Branch," although the meditating bird and the thrilling worm are given a faint human quality. Metaphor, however, dominates the poem. One might call the whole work an extended metaphor in which the speaker is the deciduous branch and the falling leaves those elements of character or habit that he discards. The verbs *coils* and *will glide* (lines 1 and 2) reveal a submerged metaphor in which winter = snake. And the verb *pick* (line 8) reveals another submerged metaphor in which eye = carrion bird. Stripping *summer to seed* requires that the reader equate summer with a plant from which flowers and fruit are stripped away, leaving only the seed that looks lifeless but is the germinating source for new life.

In addition to those figures of speech that connect two images (eye = carrion bird) and those that connect an abstraction with an image (summer = plant), the poem uses various verbal devices that incorporate a double idea. The word *sun* (line 10) is probably a pun, urging the reader also to think of *son,* the *promised son,* i.e. Jesus; this suggestion is strengthened by the whole concept of Christian renewal after death. *Trunk* (line 23) has many meanings, all of them useful here— the trunk of a tree, the human body, a container for stuff, the container for the body as perishable stuff, i.e. coffin. And the poem's final word, *evergreen* is another pun, meaning both "a non-deciduous tree" and, if broken into two words, "always fresh or alive."

There is hyperbole implicit in *on every bough* (line 3) and understatement in the word *worm* for the devil in serpent form. Finally, the poem depends heavily on an appreciation of paradox. The conventional Christian paradox of dying in order to live is related to the metaphor of the deciduous branch that can, miraculously, become "ever green" and to the psychological idea of casting off the old self to become something new and more permanent. Within this larger framework, the paradox of nourishing perishable stuff to its rot is a smaller motif. One nourishes the body to keep it from rotting; but living, including nourishment, uses up that body and hastens it towards death; yet this very rot is a way of cleaning out what is perishable in favor of the tough and final growth. The contradictions are all resolvable.

Figurative language and circuitous ways of saying things can have opposite uses in different kinds of poems. The poet who seeks to compress much meaning into a few words uses figurative language to suggest additional ideas and feelings that are not directly stated. The poet who wishes to elaborate, to pursue his meaning to its farthest verbal limits, can use figurative language for achieving varied and forceful detail.

JOURNAL PROJECTS

43. Write two quatrains, either serious poems or examples of light verse, one of which is dependent on overstatement, one on understatement.
44. Try to write a short poem, using any form you like, that includes at least one piece of verbal irony. Are you able to indicate ironic intent in a way that will convey your meaning to your reader? How can you manage to do this?
45. Plan a poem that uses dramatic irony. Work out a real event or situation. Then devise a special character as the speaker of the poem who will present the event or situation in his own, some-

what distorted, way. How will you help the reader to recognize that this character's view is not accurate?

46. Return to your sonnet (Projects #12, #24, #30, #34) and your persuasive poem in free verse (Projects #7, #16, #24, #30, #35) to examine the figurative language you have used. In each poem, are the figures of speech and circuitous verbal devices compatible among themselves? Are any non-literal expressions either too familiar to be interesting or too private to be clear?

APPRAISING AND REVISING

MEASURING THE POEM
AGAINST FIRST PLANS

It is unfortunate that books like this one have to be written so that one topic follows another, as though the process of writing a poem were a linear sequence of activities. The process of appraisal, treated here in the third section, is really going on all the while a poem is being made. Rejecting an idea, deciding on a suitable form, rearranging lines or stanzas, changing one word for another, crossing out passages that seem unessential, worrying that a figure isn't clear or that the wrong connotation has crept into a phrase—all these are the poet's appraisals of his work-in-progress. Whether they take days of deliberate work or are instant, subconscious feelings about "rightness," they monitor his progress as he goes, warning him against digression, obscurity, bad taste, verbosity, inappropriateness, and rewarding him for expressions and arrangements that seem suitable.

Thoughtful writing always includes simultaneous evaluation. But the intense and undiluted force of a poet's critical faculties ought finally to focus on the completed poem. In most cases, if the poet is intelligent, imaginative, and rigorous in self-criticism, he will discover that what he took to be a finished poem isn't finished at all. Indeed, it may turn out to be a dozen drafts away from the final poem.

Appraisal and revision are not easy. They sometimes seem less interesting, more tedious than getting an idea and putting the poem together. And they ask the poet to penetrate his defenses, to recognize that he may have written something dull or silly or muddled. It may be comforting to the working poet to look at preliminary drafts of some splendid poems, evidence that even eminent authors make faulty judgments during the writing process. Here is an early version of Robert Frost's "Design" (p. 41), then called "In White":

In White

A dented spider like a snow drop white
On a white Heal-all, holding up a moth
Like a white piece of lifeless satin cloth—
Saw ever curious eye so strange a sight?—
Portent in little, assorted death and blight
Like the ingredients of a witches' broth?—
The beady spider, the flower like a froth,
And the moth carried like a paper kite.

What had that flower to do with being white,
The blue prunella every child's delight?
What brought the kindred spider to that height?
(Make we no thesis of the miller's plight.)
What but design of darkness and of night?
Design, design! Do I use the word aright?

A useful way for a poet to begin an orderly evaluation is to look at this poem carefully in the light of the intentions he had when he started to work on it. If the poem has been conceived and developed within a few days, this will not be difficult. But if it has been months or years in the making, the poet will wish to look back to his first jottings to refresh his memory about what he started out to do. (This is one good reason for keeping all work sheets, even the most ragged and primitive.) A check against early plans can reveal some surprises. The poem that set out to be descriptive may have turned philosophic, focusing on a complicated idea. The poet who had intended to persuade a reader towards some attitude may discover that he has, instead, poured out intense feelings that are too specifically personal to be persuasive. The restraints of wit may have been transformed to emotional involvement, the literal event into a metaphor for some abstraction.

A divergence from early plans is no mark of failure. Writing a poem is not merely the recording of organized thought and language but a way of organizing both together. A poem may be better because it changes or transcends the poet's original plan. But it is not necessarily better, and this is what the poet needs to judge as he measures his poem against his first intentions.

If the poem has enlarged its scope, the statement it makes may be more significant. The observation that first seemed attractive for its own sake may have become representative of a general theme, so that the work is given more stature. Sometimes ideas that started or could have started as separate poems become intermingled, and their new relationship may be strikingly original. Randall Jarrell, in an essay describing the development of "The Woman at the Washington Zoo," explains how several threads—exotic Indian women wearing saris, drab government secretaries, the animals in the zoo, and old folk tales about animals—were eventually synthesized into a poem. The poem is remarkably unified and original.*

Sometimes a poet's divergence from his plan leads to an unsatisfying poem. The excitement of working with words and images can lure the writer into a cul-de-sac so that his poem becomes distended with digression and overelaboration. If he finds that one section of the poem comes easily but then

---

* The essay appears in *Understanding Poetry*, 3rd edition, by Cleanth Brooks and Robert Penn Warren, Holt, Rinehart and Winston, Inc., 1960.

becomes impatient with the difficulties of another part, the final work may be unbalanced; the poem with too rapid, too weak, too insipid an ending for its beginning is one familiar distortion. He may push description or example too hard towards a theme and so make the poem ponderous. Or he may drift away from seriousness into wit with disastrous results.

Here are two versions of a poem by James Joyce (1882–1941) that retained the same size and shape in revision. The author's original intention, though, seems to have changed in an important way:

Ruminants

He travels after the wintry sun,
Driving the cattle along the straight red road;
Calling to them in a voice they know.
He drives the cattle above Cabra.

His voice tells them home is not far.
They low and make soft music with their hoofs.
He drives them without labor before him,
Steam pluming their foreheads.

Herdsman, careful of the herd,
Tonight sleep well by the fire
When the herd too is asleep
And the door made fast.

*Tilly**

He travels after a winter sun,
Urging the cattle along a cold red road,
Calling to them, a voice they know,
He drives his beasts above Cabra.

* "Tilly" is an Irish expression for the thirteenth item in a set (the extra piece in a baker's dozen). This poem became the thirteenth poem in a small collection by Joyce called *Pomes Penyeach* (1927).

> The voice tells them home is warm.
> They moo and make brute music with their hoofs.
> He drives them with a flowering branch before him,
> Smoke pluming their foreheads.
>
> Boor, bond of the herd,
> Tonight stretch full by the fire!
> I bleed by the black stream
> For my torn bough!

James Joyce started out with an impersonal voice for his poem. The poet is "outside," reporting and interpreting slightly. The final version begins in the same way, but, in the last stanza, reveals a first-person voice, not the poet's but the invented voice of the injured tree. What improvements this change provides! The whole poem seems more enclosed, since the voice belongs within the scene itself, and more interesting because that voice reveals an original and unexpected attitude towards the episode. Furthermore, feeling is intensified because the voice belongs to a sufferer rather than to an observer. Finally, the theme is enlarged. An event that seemed happy and bucolic in the first version becomes more complicated: carefree simplicity is also rude and thoughtless; the rewards of rest after work are accompanied by some loss and ruin. Various changes in vocabulary accompany the new point of view. *Cattle* (in line 4) becomes *beasts, soft music* becomes *brute music,* changes towards less favorable connotations that indicate a plant's alien view of the animal kingdom, a kingdom to which the *herdsman* turned *boor* belongs. The vocabulary becomes "easier," less dependent on knowledge beyond the scene, and more suited to the "thoughts" of a tree: *low* turns to *moo; steam* to *smoke; sleep* (a concept a plant would not "know about") to *stretch*.

The novice poet in the midst of revisions may be further

helped through reading another poem, "The Kraken," in many
ways memorable, but a poem that looks as though its author
Tennyson swerved from his original plan with resulting loss:

The Kraken

Below the thunders of the upper deep,
Far, far beneath in the abysmal sea,
His ancient, dreamless, uninvaded sleep
The Kraken sleepeth: faintest sunlights flee
About his shadowy sides, above him swell
Huge sponges of millennial growth and height;
And far away into the sickly light,
From many a wondrous grot and secret cell
Unnumbered and enormous polypi
Winnow with giant arms the slumbering green.
There hath he lain for ages, and will lie
Battening upon huge sea worms in his sleep,
Until the latter fire shall heat the deep;
Then once by man and angels to be seen,
In roaring he shall rise and on the surface die.

—Alfred, Lord Tennyson (1809–1892)

These lines about a mythical monster have a haunting quality, but the reader is left with a strange sense of mixed intentions. The most intriguing part of the poem's meaning and
what appears to have been the original point of departure is
the concept that the ancient pagan beast is not dead but
sleeping and will rise again on the Christian Judgment Day.
This is a provocative idea—that old beliefs as well as the
souls of dead mortals will be called up for a final cataclysmic
muster. But Tennyson seems to have been diverted by the
visual details of the Kraken on the ocean floor. Much of the
poem is given over to such description which, though mysteri-
ous and beautiful, does not really fortify the idea of the final

rising. Divided almost equally between idea and extravagant description, the poem founders somewhat, and the reader wonders, "What was the author meaning to do?"

Tennyson's problem was, in some ways, the very problem that must have faced Robert Frost in writing "Design" (p. 41). That poem, too, is an "idea" poem that also involves description. The difference is that Frost's descriptive details are more closely related to the poem's idea. Their balanced suggestions of beauty and horror, innocence and evil are connotatively connected with the large question the poem raises, so that description is always subordinate to idea. Whereas Tennyson's *wondrous grot, enormous polypi, huge sea worms* have no links with Judgment Day, Frost's *rigid satin cloth, witches' broth,* and other phrases suggest the possibility of evil design within a picture of natural beauty.

It is probable that departures from the original plan, like other kinds of revision, more often make the poem better than worse. Checking the "finished" poem against the first plan, though, will give the writer a chance to measure the distance between them and to decide whether he has indeed moved forward.

JOURNAL PROJECTS

47. Examine again these poems on which you've been working and consult your original notes about each: the persuasive poem (Projects #7, #16, #24, #30, #35, #46); the sonnet (Projects #12, #24, #30, #34, #46); the triolet (Project #18); the extended metaphor or simile (Project #42). Measure each "finished" poem against your earliest plans, asking those questions that are appropriate.

a. Is the process with which I started (narration, description, or development of an idea) still the process of the poem? Is that process clearly dominant? If the process has changed, has the

change been carried far enough to avoid a sense of mixed intentions?

b. Have I fulfilled the purpose I had in mind when I began the
poem? If not, is that because I haven't been able to implement my purpose or because I've changed my mind about the
poem's purpose? If there has been a change, is it a useful one?

c. Does the form assigned or chosen still seem right for the material? Would a change of form lead to improvement?

d. Are the point of view and the voice of the poem the same as
they were at the start? Have I considered other possibilities?
Are the present point of view and voice those I really want?

𝕏 *BREAKING FREE OF MODELS*

A few poets seem to know from the first what they want to say and how they want to say it. They progress from poem to poem, consolidating their ideas, refining and sharpening their own unique modes of expression, their personal style. For most, though, the path is not so direct. The typical poet's first wish to write poems is somewhat unfocused, an urge he cannot quite understand. He knows that poetry is the medium he wants to use, but he's not sure why his instincts choose it from among all the ways of expression. The influence of someone else—a teacher, a colleague, a poet he admires—is often important in this early, uncertain stage. Perhaps that influence is responsible for his wish to write. Or he may seek guidance from outside to help him get started.

Consider this representative case. A young person reads some of E. E. Cummings's poems and admires them enough to search for more. His enthusiasm grows as he works through the Cummings canon. "This is poetry I like," he may think. "Why haven't I discovered Cummings earlier?" (Cummings is selected for this example because his poetry is unusually distinctive, recognizable, and because he has a strong appeal for some readers.) Eventually, the reader may decide that he'd like to write poems. His way of beginning will probably be to imitate Cummings.

As in other endeavors, the lessons an apprentice receives from a master can be an invaluable way of learning. The novice, already comfortable with Cummings's subjects, begins to work within the same range. He tries to use type in ways that Cummings sometimes uses it (see p. 93) and sound and rhythm as they are used in other Cummings poems. He tries to adopt the Cummings syntax with its juggled parts of speech and novel structures. He tries to achieve the élan that characterizes most Cummings poems. In the process, he can scarcely help but increase his sensitivity to sound and rhythm, his awareness of words, his ability to compress meaning into small numbers of words, his insights about his own thoughts and feelings.

But, the more he imitates, the more certainly he will discover that Cummings is distinguished because he has pushed his own kind of poetry towards its limits. The beginner, if he is realistic, becomes convinced that, no matter how his insights and skills enlarge, he will never surpass or even match his model. It is as though that particular niche for excellence had already been filled. He has, then, two choices—to continue writing second-rate Cummings or to use what he has learned to establish his own view and his own voice.

If the learning poet chooses the better path, he may not know how to make the break away from the kind of poetry he has been writing with increasing competence. One practical method is to change models abruptly, to try to write like another distinctive poet, say Dylan Thomas. Suddenly, his writing problems will all be different ones as he strives towards an expanded line, a rush of syllables that pours out of the limits of the tighter Cummings form and with a new stress pattern, towards another vocabulary, a richer diet of imagery, a different relationship with a different natural environment. Unless the learning poet is a natural mimic, he will quickly discover that he can't make these changes and give up the attempt. But sloughing off the influence of his old model and finding which characteristics of the new model are incompatible with his own capacities will help him to identify more surely what those capacities might be.

Another method is to make a radical break away from a form that has become a habit. The poet who has written reams of bad Whitman may discover that moving from free verse to more regular forms brings him nearer to his own way of writing. Or the imitator of Emily Dickinson's quatrains may find release in free verse. Shifts to new kinds of subjects, experiments with another point of view, deliberate efforts to work with a different vocabulary or syntax or rhythm—all of these changes of direction can help the learning poet declare his independence from earlier models.

The breaking away is usually uncomfortable. After the satisfying progress of his apprenticeship with its well-defined goals, the poet now finds himself insecure, fragmented, without a sense of what he ought to do. He becomes a prairie-dog poet, scurrying over the landscape, submerging himself in one area of poetry only to surface again somewhere else to repeat the process. This feeling of lost power and purpose, though, can be the prelude to a new and more permanent confidence. The poet who persists through trial and error will eventually get inklings of his own inclinations and his own strengths. When he looks carefully at his different ventures, he is likely to discover some distinctive and personal quality that emerges in various poems. It may be a tendency to write syllabic poetry, or a flair for rhyme or other sound patterns, or an interest in unusual metaphors, or an ironic view, or a sense of humor. Following whatever clues he discovers, he can experiment further, working slowly towards his own way of writing a poem.

Journal Projects

48. Try to imitate closely any poem you have read thus far in this book that is at least eight lines long. After you are satisfied that you have followed your model as carefully as you can, identify those elements in your poem that seem uncomfortably alien to your real interests and your own way of writing. Now identify anything that seems to fit your own way of writing a poem.

49. Return to your descriptive version of "Eight O'Clock" (Projects #5, #37). Have your vocabulary, feeling, and tone been obviously influenced by Housman? Do you want to liberate the poem into your own style? What changes would this liberation involve?

50. Consider again your attempt to write in the confessional "I" (Project #23). Do your lines show the influence of Maxine Kumin's model (p. 59)? How can you go about making them more your own?

SPEAKING IN THE RIGHT TONE

Unless he is communicating with himself and does not intend his lines to be shared with others, a poet sets up some sort of relationship with those who will read or hear his poem. His attitude towards his audience, as expressed or suggested in his words, is called the TONE of the poem. Every poem has a tone. If the tone seems to be neutral or unnoticeable, it is probably because the author has assumed the attitude of someone speaking to those who share his interests and has not attempted to establish a special relationship. There are various well-defined postures that a poet can assume vis-à-vis his reader; he can scold, praise, insult, tease, ridicule, curry favor, etc., and any of these can be effective in appropriate circumstances. But such emphatic attitudes are difficult to control in poetry, especially for the inexperienced writer, and should be expressed with caution.

Typically, the tone of the poem is somewhat more subtle. In "Design" (p. 41), Robert Frost offers readers the chance to speculate with him about the unusual scene he has observed; the tone is one of offering an idea to companions willing and able to absorb it and to carry it farther in their own minds. In "Coup de Grâce" (p. 128), A. D. Hope assumes that he and the reader share an amused cynicism, in contrast to those unnamed, less perceptive others who let loose *a round of ap-*

plause; this tone gently flatters the reader by treating him as one of the poet's elite colleagues.

One pitfall that a poet often faces is the temptation to be preachy and didactic, particularly if he is fervent about the value of his poem's message. This temptation is intensified by the many readers who think that a good poem is a pep talk, a vehicle for moral uplift, something to keep firm the will of the stalwart or to comfort the discouraged. Poems whose first and direct purpose is to provide such spiritual fiber may have therapeutic use, but that is quite separate from their value as poems.

Those who set out to write competent poems, as opposed to sermons or pieces of psychological support, can avoid an irritating and didactic tone by remembering their audience during all the writing and revising stages. A poet probably does best to assume that his readers or listeners, though they may be less adept than he at using words, will be his equals in intelligence and in their capacity to respond to experience. Those who lack the combination of intelligence and the aesthetic response that makes poetry interesting will probably not give any attention to his work. Condescension is not only impolite but futile.

It is helpful, too, to remember the state of the person encountering a poem. He is curled up quietly with a book or magazine; he is sitting in a public room where someone is reading aloud; he is listening to his radio or record-player. Whatever the setting, and however alert his mind to the poem itself, he is likely to be physically passive. He has, in fact, arrested other activities in the interests of poetry. In this state, with mind tuned in and muscles slack, he may be irritated if the poem imperiously exhorts him to go out and look at the moon or lead an army or tear down a building that is blighting the view somewhere else. Even though he may approve the sentiment behind such urging, his posture as reader or listener offers natural resistance to commands, making him uncomfortable, possibly negative, in his response.

There are ways of teaching, ways of exhorting the reader that are less likely to trigger this negative reaction. Some poems strike an irritating note because they are directly addressed to the reader as "you"—the reader is being talked to, talked *at* in some cases. Here are the opening lines of Longfellow's "A Psalm of Life":

> Tell me not, in mournful numbers,
>   Life is but an empty dream!—
> For the soul is dead that slumbers,
>   And things are not what they seem.

Not only is Longfellow addressing his reader directly, but he makes each reader part of a lugubrious company. Furthermore, he begins on the defensive, as though the reader has just complained that *Life is but an empty dream,* an artificial premise, a pretense that the reader rather than the writer has "caused" the poem. The poem proceeds in the manner of a lecture through its final stanza of exhortation:

> Let us, then, be up and doing,
>   With a heart for any fate;
> Still achieving, still pursuing,
>   Learn to labor and to wait.

These lines seek to urge on, to challenge the reader who is relaxing with his book. Why should he move? And, if he should be stirred to action, what is he meant to do? The instructions are vague throughout the poem, aimed at encouraging a generalized optimism that is not focused on any action or attitude more specific than *to labor and to wait,* two processes one can scarcely avoid.

Better poems use better methods. Dylan Thomas's "Do

Not Go Gentle Into That Good Night" (p. 52) forcefully
argues that the human spirit ought to resist the body's inevita-
ble mortality. But the lines are addressed to the poet's father.
This is not only appropriate but it allows the reader to occupy
a more comfortable position during the poem's urging; he over-
hears the exhortation, but is not its target. "Sailing to Byzantium" (p. 117) also teaches: man's artistic creations have
greater endurance and value than man himself. But the lesson
unfolds with Yeats as pupil, while the reader merely listens
in. "Ars Poetica" (p. 7) succeeds because MacLeish does not
address his rules for good poetry to anyone. In "The Golf
Links" (p. 131), Sarah N. Cleghorn expresses a high moral
purpose and may have meant to inspire direct action; but
the reader is merely shown a specific ironic situation and allowed to develop his own response.

To advise poets never to address the reader directly would
be as annoying to them as a preachy poem is to a reader. Used
with skill, the direct address can be effective or, at least, not
irritating. The last words of Robert Frost's "The Pasture"
are *You come too,* an invitation so gentle and attractive that
it makes the reader feel honored to be included.

Though refraining from direct address to the reader is often
an effective preventative, it does not assure that the poem will
be free of the preacher-teacher tone. "The Silver Swan" (p.
23), even with its theme cast into a rhyming fable and enunciated by an imaginary swan, sounds like a poem designed to
educate the reader about the world's sorry condition. The statement of the final line, general, without forceful images, has the
quality of a trite, instructive aphorism. In "On His Seventy-
fifth Birthday" (p. 28), Walter Savage Landor also risks annoying. The speaker's defensive generalities and lofty tone
seem to imply, "See what a noble and dedicated man I am,
much too good for this world."

All of these admonitions are meant to keep the poet from

irritating readers unintentionally. There are times, though, when he seeks an abrasive confrontation with his reader, and for such poems shock tactics like direct address, imperious commands, and the uncompromising enunciation of preferences may be useful and effective. Here is an example of the assaultive tone that characterizes some twentieth-century poetry:

The Rest

O helpless few in my country,
O remnant enslaved!

Artists broken against her,
A-stray, lost in the villages,
Mistrusted, spoken-against,

Lovers of beauty, starved,
Thwarted with systems,
Helpless against the control:

You who can not wear yourselves out
By persisting to successes,
You who can only speak,
Who can not steel yourselves into reiteration;

You of the finer sense,
Broken against false knowledge,
You who can know at first hand,
Hated, shut in, mistrusted:

Take thought:
I have weathered the storm,
I have beaten out my exile.

—Ezra Pound (1885–   )

A reader can react to this poem in one of two ways, neither of them comfortable. If he considers himself to be included within the *helpless few,* his helplessness, frustration, and sense of neglect will be newly rubbed raw. If he counts himself among the majority not addressed directly (though certainly a target of these bitter words), he will probably resent the elitist sense of righteousness under repression that Pound expresses. The reader must, in short, feel either like an early Christian on his way to the lions or like a Roman spectator angered by the martyr's smug confidence in his own superiority. This abrasive tone is entirely intentional, meant to criticize, agitate, protest against false values. Because of such direction and force, the poem is much more effective than the querulous lines of "On His Seventy-fifth Birthday," even though the feeling that impelled Landor's poem may have been quite similar to Pound's feeling.

JOURNAL PROJECTS

51. Return to Project #6, your early notes on why you wanted to write various poems. Were any of these ideas strongly motivated by your urge to teach the reader something? In development would any of these poems have acquired a didactic tone that could be irritating?

52. Look closely at the persuasive poem on which you've been working (Projects #7, #16, #24, #30, #35, #46, #47). Does it include direct address to the reader? If so, do you think that this is an effective technique? Is the tone of the poem relatively neutral or does it carry some clearly discernible attitude? What attitude? What reaction would you have to the tone if you were the reader instead of the author?

GUARDING AGAINST SENTIMENTALITY

The definitions of both "sentiment" and "sentimentality" include the word "feeling." But the two terms are very different. "Sentiment" means a feeling of any kind, and the word is connotatively of neutral value. "Sentimentality," though, has unfavorable connotations and means exaggerated feelings only of certain kinds (tenderness, sadness, joy, for example, but not anger, envy, relief), or, more often, the exaggerated expression of those feelings. Sentimentality in writing is both excessive and niggardly. It is excessive because the author reacts with more verbal show of emotion than the subject seems to warrant and expects his reader to respond with a like measure of feeling. It is niggardly because the writer fails to make the reasons for his feelings amply clear, using easy stock words and phrases to produce an automatic response. In short, the poet who proffers sentimentality is dealing in unearned emotion.

There are forms of communication in which sentimentality is intentional. The writers of some soap operas, screenplays, and song lyrics know that it is good business to release "a good cry." In these instances, the writer is entirely outside the feeling, deliberately manipulating some time-tested stimuli to produce the maximum reaction from an audience. Poets, though, are rarely tempted to these measures, since there are few rewards for bad poetry. Typically, the poet who indulges in sentimentality is sincerely moved by his subject and wants to share his feeling with the reader. He respects poetry as a medium for conveying feelings, and he tries to use it for that purpose. What turns his feelings to spun sugar on the page? How does sentiment become sentimentality?

Is the topic to blame? Not really. One can write about almost any topic with or without sentimentality. Yet there are some topics that seem already entangled in the threads of trite emotionalism—parted lovers, mothers, dead children, faithful pets, lost toys, abandoned homes, old armchairs, and all the other furniture of the nostalgic past. Sentimentality clings to topics that evoke tears of joy as well as of sorrow—babies, live children, springtime, young lovers, weddings, reunions, the recovery of what was lost. Poets cannot, nor should they try, to avoid all of these. But if a poet's work deals with one of the items in these lists, he ought to be especially sure that he is starting fresh, meticulously cutting his own idea clean from an accumulation of stale connotations.

Here are two poems that treat the same topic, the death of a dog and its effect on the boy who owned him. One poem is sticky with sentimentality; the other is not. It may be useful to search out the reasons for the difference.

Dead Dog

The boy has lost his faithful friend,
The best he's ever known;
And through the field where they both played
He wanders now alone.

No parent's comforting caress,
No new-found pet or toy
Can soothe away his bitter tears
Or turn his grief to joy.

His father dug a grave, and there
They reverently laid
The lifeless, quiet form of Pal
Beneath a willow's shade.

The boy sits near and wonders if
His absent friend awaits
The day they two will meet again
Beyond the heavenly gates.

—Anonymous

The Pardon

My dog lay dead five days without a grave
In the thick of summer, hid in a clump of pine
And a jungle of grass and honeysuckle-vine.
I who had loved him while he kept alive

Went only close enough to where he was
To sniff the heavy honeysuckle-smell
Twined with another odor heavier still
And hear the flies' intolerable buzz.

Well, I was ten and very much afraid.
In my kind world the dead were out of range
And I could not forgive the sad or strange
In beast or man. My father took the spade

And buried him. Last night I saw the grass
Slowly divide (it was the same scene
But now it glowed a fierce and mortal green)
And saw the dog emerging. I confess

I felt afraid again, but still he came
In the carnal sun, clothed in a hymn of flies,
And death was breeding in his lively eyes.
I started in to cry and call his name,

Asking forgiveness of his tongueless head.
. . . I dreamt the past was never past redeeming:

But whether this was false or honest dreaming
I beg death's pardon now. And mourn the dead.

—Richard Wilbur (1921–   )

Although both poems deal with material that can easily trigger a trite reaction, "The Pardon" demonstrates that an able poet can handle this kind of topic without being drawn into sentimentality. One way in which he achieves this is by developing an interesting complexity in the speaker. The voice belongs to the person who has suffered the loss, speaking years later. The memory of the distressing death has been changed by time, and undergoes one final change—the catharsis of a fearful dream that quiets the unresolved agonies of the years between. The poem presents in miniature a complicated psychological history—a traumatic event lodged in the subconscious to surface again after many years and to be dealt with on new terms. The speaker's accumulation of reactions is unique. The voice of "Dead Dog," on the other hand, is that of an observer outside the situation, reporting it to the reader. He has no personality that shapes the event and makes it interesting. And the event itself is described without special sensitivity so that there is little to distinguish it from any similar bereavement. The live boy and dead dog are presented in generalized outline without those special details that would show the uniqueness of their relationship. How was Pal unlike other dogs? How did he look and act in life and in death? Are the boy's tears the result only of loneliness, or are fear, anger, resentment part of his reaction?

How much does the form of "Dead Dog" contribute to its sentimentality? Its alternating tetrameter and trimeter lines, rhyming *abcb*, seem to have a singsong, monotonous rhythm that accentuates triteness. But, before ascribing too much blame to the poem's formal characteristics, one might look again at Wordsworth's "A Slumber Did My Spirit Seal"

(p. 28), another poem about death and bereavement in a pattern rather like "Dead Dog"; the Wordsworth poem, though, is much less sentimental. Obviously, form is not the whole problem in "Dead Dog," although the regularity of the rhythm and the awful inevitability of the uninspired rhyming pairs enhance the insipid effect.

Ultimately, it is in the words that the sentimentality of "Dead Dog" rests. The poem lacks any engaging diction. What is more, *faithful friend, bitter tears, heavenly gates* have been so over-used that they have lost whatever vitality they once owned. Clichés like these are the stock in trade of the sentimentalist, counterfeit coins that may mechanically buy an impressionable reader's response but will not bear scrutiny. The poem includes no redeeming originalities in figures of speech. When language like this is cut to fit a familiar form like the ballad stanza that is kept absolutely regular, all iambs from start to finish, the result is trivial and boring.

In contrast, the language that Richard Wilbur uses in "The Pardon" is original and evocative. *Kind world, fierce and mortal green, carnal sun, hymn of flies, lively eyes, tongueless head* distinguish the event from others like it in both literal description and figurative language. The death and its aftermath become personal, unique, memorable. There is nothing difficult or puzzling about the language of "The Pardon"; every word is entirely clear. But the force with which the expressions impress themselves attests to the poet's care in choosing and arranging them to give this poem its remarkable quality. In "The Pardon," the point of view is interesting, the form does not protrude and embarrass, the language is distinctive. The poet's expression of feeling is not excessive, but qualified by the passage of time and an adult perspective. And it is not niggardly; those fears felt at the death and afterwards are justified by valid and detailed explanation.

Journal Projects

53. Return to Project #2, your early notes on the origins of ideas for poems. Did any of these ideas start with observations, memories, or feelings that would have led towards a sentimental treatment? If so, think further about the idea and try to plan a presentation that would avoid sentimentality.

54. Examine the metaphors for death you composed for Project #40. Do any of these have sentimental qualities? Why?

55. Look again at your sonnet (Projects #12, #24, #30, #34, #46, #47). Has use of a conventional form made your treatment of the subject conventional? Have you used any tired language? Are there changes that would make your view of the subject more complex and original, your language more distinctive? If you feel that your sonnet has become a poem in which you are patching the patches, abandon it and begin a new one.

GETTING RID OF RHETORIC

One quality that distinguishes good poetry is its economy. A good poem compresses into the best words content that would require a lengthy paraphrase in less carefully organized language. It conveys a sense impression, a feeling, an idea quickly and forcefully by using words packed with meaning and by avoiding the distractions of extra verbiage. Superfluous language in a bad poem is sometimes just dull padding to fill out the meter or to explicate what better words could show. Sometimes, though, it is extravagantly ornamental, more elaborate or impassioned or exalted than the subject deserves, and burdens the poem with empty rhetoric.

Mark Twain, for Chapter 17 of *Adventures of Huckleberry Finn,* constructed a flagrant example of the rhetorical poem called "Ode to Stephen Dowling Bots, Dec'd." His lines are about a boy who fell into a well and drowned, a fate revealed only in the penultimate stanza. Before the reader is told how the child died, the poem raises and answers a series of rhetorical questions. Four stanzas are spun out to establish that he didn't expire from whooping cough, measles, a broken heart, or a stomach ailment, the lines made even sillier by a sequence of rhymes for *Bots*. Mark Twain was, of course, exaggerating the faults of rhetorical poetry to emphasize his point. Bad poems are rarely quite so bad. But they share the same tend-

ency towards language inflated to confer dignity on a subject
or to demonstrate the writer's learning.

Sentimentality, discussed in the last section, is one kind of
rhetoric, but there are many kinds. The following topical poem
suggests the way rhetoric invades a poem, the forms it takes,
and its dismal effects:

The Beelah Viaduct

O wondrous age! a wondrous age we live in,
 When Stainmore echoes with the awful din;
What novel sounds the eighty men are giving,
 While fixing firm the iron pillars in . . .

All hail to Steam! all hail to men of Brain,
 Who sweep all obstacles before them,
Cut down the hills, and through the mountains bore,
 And make admiring crowds adore them . . .

"The cloud-cap't Towers, the solemn Temples,"
 (As Shakespeare tells us in his verse sublime)
Our Bridge at last shall crumble—pass away—
 When there shall also be an end of Time.

Nay, "the great Globe itself," he plainly says,
 Shall disappear, and then be seen no more;
We don't believe this creed—our world will still
 Move round the sun as she hath done before.

But when "The Archangel's trump shall sound"
 (As good John Wesley piously sings),
May we among the heavenly host be found,
 When we have bid farewell to earthly things.

        —John Close (1816–1891)

John Close was apparently moved to write these lines by
watching the building of a bridge. This activity could be the
topic for a good poem if the poet's special perception and treat-

ment were to present the building in an imaginative way—by developing its relationship to some event in myth or history, by exploring the gains or losses of the technology it represents, by making it the metaphor for some quest or accomplishment. Close's poem suggests that he may have entertained each of these ideas fleetingly, but no one idea is sustained long enough to make a point. Around the central vacuum where the real subject should be, he has arranged exclamations like *O wondrous age!* and *All hail to Steam!* They express some kind of intensity, but since the idea they embellish is never clear, one wonders whether that intensity is ironic or genuinely enthusiastic.

The guise of excitement, then, doesn't seem to cover any substance. The language is hollow. But, to bolster up the whole effect, the author introduces some learned allusions. Why is Shakespeare (or, to be more accurate, Prospero) quoted? Only so that his *creed* can be refuted. But even the refutation doesn't seem to lead anywhere except to another quotation, this one by John Wesley, also useless. Although it is not rejected, the quotation has nothing really to do with the poem. The author is obviously not sure of what he wants to say and has tried to compensate with exalted and erudite expression. But the words themselves so clutter the work that it becomes even more difficult to identify a glimmering of the poet's meaning. What is the theme? That man through invention and technology can improve the world? That men may labor but the fruits of their work will pass? That what man makes is more permanent than man himself? That material progress is a pale precursor of eternal spiritual value? That man's efforts mar the landscape? The reader cannot decide. All he can discover is that a bridge was constructed with massive technological effort, but he could have learned that more emphatically from a news report.

It is, of course, easier to find another poet's rhetorical excesses than one's own. But there are some warning signs that a writer can look for when he is reviewing and appraising his poem. If he is honest with himself, he will know whether the subject of the poem is still really interesting to him. If it is not, he is especially vulnerable to the temptation of trying to make it seem more interesting through overblown language. Probably he should put the poem aside, forever or until he becomes genuinely intrigued with it. If he still has a valid interest in the poem, he will want to make certain that this has been communicated without bombast, pretension, or sentimentality.

Do the lines contain overstatements that are not recognizable figures but are deceptive? (A man does not expect to be taken literally when he says that his neighbor is as rich as Croesus, but, if he inflates his neighbor's annual income from thirty to thirty-five thousand dollars, he offers overstatement as fact.) Are the figurative images too grand for their associations? (To treat a canoe's collision with a submerged stump like the sinking of the *Titanic* would be excessive.) Is the vocabulary too formal and erudite for the topic of the poem and for the author's feelings? (If one can reasonably call a spade a spade, it is pretentious to talk about "an implement forged from iron to lift the turf.") Does the poem include rhetorical questions that take up space without furthering the idea? Or rhetorical variations on a theme in which a single thought is stated, then restated in different words, then, perhaps, restated again? Are there interjections like *Alas!, Oh!, Terrible to tell!, Hurrah!* used as metrical fillers or in the hope of stirring up emotions? Are exclamation marks lavished about in an attempt to promote breathless wonder? In most cases, these features will not survive incisive examination, and their loss is not regrettable. Getting rid of rhetoric is a double process—the pruning away of useless and excessive language, and the altering of what is kept so that the freight of meaning each word carries is appropriate, solid, and balanced.

JOURNAL PROJECTS

56. Return to Projects #8, #9, #14, #15, the same material used for blank verse, couplets, quatrains, and free verse. In working with any of these forms, have you allowed extra rhetoric to enter the poem? If you have, can you make useful changes without abandoning the form?

57. Again examine your persuasive poem (Projects #7, #16, #24, #30, #35, #46, #47, #52) with special attention to its language. Have you depended on any extra or inflated expressions to convince your audience? Have you made digressions that are pedantic? Is any of your syntax or vocabulary pretentious? Can you make changes in the interests of economy and more honest expression?

58. Reconsider your attempt to write in the confessional "I" (Projects #23, #50). Has the personal nature of the exercise tempted you to any rhetorical excesses? Can you translate your feelings into more compressed, more meaningful language?

MAKING JUDGMENTS
ABOUT OBSCURITY

Most of those who work at writing poetry and hope to see it published have faced a chilling question in the middle of the night, sometimes in the middle of a line: "Who will read it?" The suspicion that an important and carefully expressed communication will not reach its audience is their most frustrating occupational hazard.

A resurgence of interest in poetry in recent years has not really alleviated the anxieties of the writer struggling with his poem. He recognizes that much (though not all) of this new enthusiasm is for poetry that is spoken and listened to, with or without musical accompaniment, in settings that emphasize spontaneity and expressiveness, where communication between poet and audience depends upon the total environment as much as upon the poem itself. Such settings are certainly appropriate for poetry, and they suggest the tradition of the troubadours and the balladeers. But they are more hospitable to the single performance than to the poem that goes through cumulative stages of composition and revision, is written down to be read and reread. The lines delivered in a coffee house or park or mixed-media entertainment are often presented as "now" expressions, valid only for the occasion. In such an atmosphere, the audience is likely to be predisposed towards accepting the poem. Written down to be read later, the same lines often provide an embarrassing demonstration that enthusiasm and sincerity are not enough to make a poem that deserves to last through time. Such lines might be called "disposable poetry."

Of more concern to a typical poet is the knowledge that the majority of readers, even those who read voluminously, are not reading contemporary poetry. Why, he wonders, do so many who like imaginative literature turn first to fiction? The usual answer is that people don't understand modern poetry.

If the synapse between poet and reader has become disconnected, this is not exclusively the fault of the poet. Modern poetry seems difficult to some readers because they are out of the habit of reading poetry. Their understanding and appreciation may have ossified at the level attained in their last literature course. Meanwhile, poetry has evolved in its own array of new habits. So when the unpracticed reader confronts a contemporary poem, even a very good one, he may object to its obscurity.

This is not altogether an inaccurate judgment. A modern poem of quality has certain obscurities because it is modern, because it is a poem, because it has quality. Twentieth-century readers do not welcome explicitness as warmly as readers in earlier times; they know more and wish to be allowed to make inferences. Where the Victorian novelist crammed his stories with detailed characters and situations, a modern novelist drops hints and oblique suggestions. Relying on what psychology and his experience with real life and fiction have taught him, the reader fills in the picture for himself. And so the modern poet is likely to suggest what his predecessors might have described. Trouble arises with readers who, though up-to-date with novels, have not moved beyond the demands of Victorian poetry.

Then, too, a poem, just by being a poem, is obscure in the

same sense (though not the same way) as an algebraic formula or a diagram: one has to know something about the conventions of its language to grasp the meaning. If the reader tackles a metaphor with scientific literalness, or insists on assigning "first definitions" from the dictionary to all words, or fails to "hear" the beat or the assonance in a line, he might as well stare at a page of Sanskrit. Poetry is in the same language as many less imaginative communications, but it uses that language with differences: the multiple meaning may enrich rather than muddle; what is factually false may be sensuously or emotionally true; the sound may be part of the meaning. The poem that is as straightforward, as uninviting of inference or imagination, as neglectful of sound, as mistake-proof as the recipe for a chocolate cake is not likely to be a good poem.

All this does not absolve the poet from concerns about obscurity. To retreat into a totally private language with the excuse that only an elite audience can be expected to understand him is self-defeating. It is not the readers but the poet who decides to send the message, and his is the major responsibility for its clarity. Though some measure of obscurity may be acceptable, indeed useful, his poem should in one sense be very clear. It should communicate forcefully at least some of his own intellectual and emotional excitement. If there are mysteries in the poem, they should not be puzzles the reader cannot hope to solve, but secrets that he will enjoy discovering. The poem should be a special communication, a compressed link between the large thoughts of its maker and the large thoughts of the reader, a point at which they touch and empathize.

It is useful for the poet to be conscious of the various ways in which he risks being obscure, not necessarily so that he will always avoid them, but so that he can more accurately judge the point at which a useful translucence turns to opacity. The simplest place to begin is with vocabulary. A poet rarely commits the error of using a word to which he ascribes an inaccurate denotation. Words that baffle the reader are usually those that are rarely used, those for which the dictionary gives several definitions that are not mutually compatible, those with connotations for the poet that may be very different from the reader's connotations. If the poet uses a foreign word, a coined word, an archaic word, a term from a special regional, professional, or ethnic vocabulary, he ought to provide enough guidance in the word's context to help the reader surmise the meaning. In "Design" (p. 41), Robert Frost talks of a *heal-all,* a homely label in some regions for the plant called prunella. This is too special to be widely understood, and some anthologists provide a footnote. Frost probably wanted *heal-all* because of its benign connotations so that he could combine them with other, malignant connotations for the peculiar mix that permeates the poem. Committed to a difficult word, he has done his best to make it plain that he is talking about a flower, even to the point of saying so in line 9. Somewhat less clearly explained is the word *property* in the third line of "Coup de Grâce" (p. 128). Readers sometimes take this to refer to real estate rather than to a theatrical property and thereby fail to perceive that the events of the poem are presented as though artificially staged.

A poet is least able to insure against the obscurities that arise from differences in connotation because it is difficult to predict the attitudes that readers have towards words. If he uses Helen of Troy as a symbol of beauty but his readers think principally of adultery and a long war, the meaning of his poem may be muddled or distorted. If he uses *chain* to signify a meaningful sequence of links but his readers conjure up images of shackles or leashes, he may fail to make his point. In respect to connotation, a poet cannot thoroughly avoid inappropriate reactions from some readers, the results of their private experi-

ences. But he can try to prevent general misunderstanding by
thinking carefully about all the possibilities latent in every
word he uses.

Between vocabulary that is unmistakably clear and that
which is likely to be obscure lies the interesting area of ambiguity, offering the poet rich possibilities for compressing more
meaning into his poem. Robert Frost's vocabulary in "Design"
(p. 41) has already been mentioned for its skillful exploitation
of ambiguities, words that entail different, sometimes opposed,
meanings. A poet is lucky to discover a word with more
than one meaning, denotative, connotative, or both, if all the
meanings are appropriate for his poem. The word *light* in line
13 of "Richard Cory" (p. 78) is such a word. What exactly
does *So on we worked, and waited for the light* mean? Is it
daylight, or the light that is turned on at the end of the working
day, or the glow that Richard Cory casts when he appears, or
the enlightenment of better social conditions, or the light of
heaven when a life of labor is done? One can vacillate endlessly
among these and other meanings. The richness of the word,
though, lies in the suitability of all the meanings. The reader
need never fix upon one; whichever way he turns, there is an
interesting possibility, and such multiplicity enriches the poem.

In this discussion of obscurity, it may be useful once again
to mention syntax. Syntax is a system of conventions govern-
ing the way words are arranged so that the logical relationships
among the things they represent can be communicated. Syntax
assists the process of putting the logic of thoughts into words.
The logic of a poet's thought may, of course, be unconventional, very different from the prose writer's. Even if it is the
same, a poet has the license to use an unconventional syntax
for putting his thoughts into words. Yet his needs vis-à-vis the
reader are the same as the prose writer's—to use a syntax
that will convey his idea. His syntax may be innovative in any

way he likes, so long as readers are able to grasp the kinds of relationships he intends.

Obscurity may arise through inversions of usual order, through elisions of elements that would normally appear in a prose sentence, through the transferring of the functions of one part of speech to another, and through the substitution of typographical relationships for the usual syntactical relationships between words. All of these can be legitimate within the poem's own syntax, but the poet needs to establish that new pattern if his meaning is to be clear. Cummings's poem about fog (p. 93), for example, violates conventions of both syntax and typography, but his new system has its own authority and, for the reader who is willing to meet the poem halfway, considerable clarity.

Using an esoteric allusion or reference is another way in which the poet sometimes becomes obscure. A poem that leans upon implications about something known only to a handful of specialists may confuse many readers. Sometimes, though, a topic that is beyond the range of general knowledge seems so useful for a poem that the writer will risk it anyway, supplying an epigraph or footnote or other apparatus to help his readers. Through these "extras," the poet at least avoids being misunderstood, but the poem that needs the help of footnotes may seem to be trailing threads and patches that should have been worked into its content. T. S. Eliot's "The Waste Land" is an eminent example of a poem that depends on footnotes to help the reader understand. For so major a work, one is probably willing to skip back and forth between text and notes in order to work out the meaning. Most poems, particularly shorter poems, cannot safely demand this effort. The author may prefer, therefore, to deal with the difficult reference within the body of the poem by providing contextual explanation.

A previous section has already mentioned some cases where

a lack of absolute clarity in a figure of speech can enrich the poem by allowing the reader to consider several appropriate meanings, e.g. Sylvia Plath's symbol in "Mushrooms" (p. 113). Sometimes the poet can attain a comparable enrichment by using an image that can be read literally or as a metaphor. Most readers, for example, seem to accept Marianne Moore's "To a Steam Roller" (p. 65) as a descriptive poem about a real steam roller. Some others, though, see the steam roller as the metaphor for an insensitive, brash, and overwhelming person; the butterfly, as a delicate companion or detail of dress. The poem is impressive when read in either of these ways. Its ambiguity is a benefit.

Problems of inverse obscurity arise with a certain kind of contemporary poem, the kind that contains less than meets the eye. Here is an absurd and exaggerated example:

> A goldfinch flies into my garden,
> So gold against the green,
> So gold against the white roses.
> Why has he come?

Why indeed? And why was this poem written? There are three images leading to a question that implies some purposeful reflection, but the nature of that reflection is vaporish. One suspects that it may lead nowhere. The diction of the poem is not remarkable in any way. The "action" of the poem is insufficient to qualify as narrative. Failing to perceive an idea, a feeling, a memorable description, or a meaningful event, the reader, particularly if he lacks confidence in his ability to understand poetry, may assume that he has somehow missed the point, that he isn't clever enough or sensitive enough to respond. Perhaps more readers should stiffen their backbones when they confront such poems and declare openly that the emperor isn't wearing any clothes. A reader has the right to expect aesthetic pleasure or meaning in a poem, preferably both. The poet who exploits this expectation by pretending that minutiae are compressed significances contributes to the obscurity that divides readers and writers like a barren no man's land. Preventing this kind of obscurity is essentially a challenge to the poet's ability to be honest with himself. Has he something to say? Has he said it or at least suggested it in a way that will invite useful inference? Or has he merely taken a fragmentary observation or idea, divided it into lines, and passed it off as a poem in the hope that he can intimidate diffident readers?

All of these ways of being obscure—through vocabulary, syntax, allusions and references, pretenses at significance— can be kept within manageable bounds by the poet who is honest, imaginative, and careful. The most challenging kind of obscurity, though, is unavoidable and is of positive value. Most competent poets have an unusual gift for casting familiar experience into unique and memorable language. Those few who are more than competent are often original thinkers; they have extraordinary ideas or see new configurations in what is around them. It is not only their sensitivity and their language that are engaging but the very texture of thought that en- genders the poem. Confronted with such a poem, the reader may well be baffled, as he would be baffled by a new scientific hypothesis or a new philosophy. The first reading may leave him troubled and uncertain about everything the poem con- tains. He will need to return to the poem several times to understand it. Indeed it may take a generation before under- standing catches up with the advanced imagination of the poet. The history of English poetry includes various examples of poems that seemed deeply obscure to readers when they were first written but which later generations found easier, and some are still being probed for meaning. Yeats's "Sailing to Byzantium" (p. 117) is now understood by most careful readers; but his later treatment of some of the same material in "Byzantium" is still a problem poem, haunting, exciting, but not yet very clear. Here is a poem that demands several readings but, even so, remains rather hard to fathom:

A High-Toned Old Christian Woman

Poetry is the supreme fiction, madame.
Take the moral law and make a nave of it
And from the nave build haunted heaven. Thus,
The conscience is converted into palms,
Like windy citherns hankering for hymns.
We agree in principle. That's clear. But take
The opposing law and make a peristyle,
And from the peristyle project a masque
Beyond the planets. Thus, our bawdiness,
Unpurged by epitaph, indulged at last,
Is equally converted into palms,
Squiggling like saxophones. And palm for palm,
Madame, we are where we began. Allow,
Therefore, that in the planetary scene
Your disaffected flagellants, well-stuffed,
Smacking their muzzy bellies in parade,
Proud of such novelties of the sublime,
Such tink and tank and tunk-a-tunk-tunk,
May, merely may, madame, whip from themselves
A jovial hullabaloo among the spheres.
This will make widows wince. But fictive things
Wink as they will. Wink most when widows wince.

—Wallace Stevens (1879–1955)

These difficult lines use an easy syntax. No reader is likely to get lost trying to thread his way through the grammar of any of the sentences. The logic of language is one that readers are used to, and it is made even more familiar by the interjected addresses to *madame* and the apparatus of rational argument leading, step by step, to a proof. But this look of ease is illusory. The vocabulary is difficult. *Fiction* seems to mean much more than it usually does, to rest heavily on the idea of "something made" in the Latin root, *facio*. *Masque* suggests a Jacobean entertainment combining music, poetry, and spectacle for amateur performers, in which the audience joined the "actors"; but how does it really fit in here? Are *nave, palms, hymns,* and *masque* intended as puns? What connotations for *windy, hankering, disaffected,* and *wink* will help the reader to establish meaning? Is Stevens deliberately entangling meaning in sound play? The complicated metaphor involving *nave* and *peristyle* requires that one understand something about church architecture. Yet, even with the help of a cathedral diagram, it is difficult to visualize or "feel" the comparison. Most baffling of all is the basic idea of the poem. What is the exact relationship among Christianity, poetry, *the moral law,* and the unspecified *opposing law* that the poem sets up? What does Wallace Stevens mean? The language is so interesting, the metaphor so controlled, the argument so sustained that it is obvious that the poem has a truth to reveal. But the reader must labor long for revelation, referring to the whole canon of Stevens's poetry for clues. Such labor is worthwhile; even if he never reaches a complete comprehension of the poem, the reader's understanding will grow with each encounter.

JOURNAL PROJECTS

59. Reread "Sonnet 73" (p. 30), "A Weaver of Carpets" (p. 70), "The Descent" (p. 101), and "Sailing to Byzantium" (p. 117). When you first read each of these, did it seem obscure? Is it still obscure? What was or is the source of your confusion? If you now understand the poem, what made it become clear for you?

BEGINNING WELL, ENDING WELL

The beginning and the end of a poem are always problem points, possibly because of a carry-over from instructions about how to write essays or other pieces of expository prose. Most people who work with words have been disciplined at an early age to the outline that reads "Introduction, Body, Conclusion," and the effects of this logical arrangement can be stultifying in poetry. A poet has an idea, a topic shaped into his own subject by his special perception and feeling, and he wants to express it. The expository sequence is not necessarily part of his concern, yet sometimes he feels that it ought to be. In terms of structure of the finished work, it would be helpful if more poets thought of themselves as fiction writers rather than as presenters of fact or opinion. A story can begin at the beginning, in the middle, or at the end, or it can jump back and forth to accord with whatever calendar the author devises. So can a poem.

The poems of beginners often are marred by introduction— a stanza, say, to set the scene, to make a generalization, to provide something familiar as a springboard for what is new. Once this is out of the way, the poem reaches the point where the poet's interest really begins and gathers momentum. Lopping off the beginning entirely, or tucking it in at a later point, often results in a strengthened poem. Even the poet who has not labored to achieve an introduction will find it useful to try beginning his poem in different places. A poet may be rigid about what he assumes to be the "natural" order for a poem, but what seems natural may really only be the order first conceived. Many poems are able to withstand some juggling without losing their clarity or balance.

The first line of a poem ought to have the strength that comes from engaging the reader's attention appropriately. "Appropriately" is an important qualification. One can, perhaps, arouse curiosity by beginning with, "What shakes my roots and makes my branches glad?" but if all that follows is a rather conventional description of spring, the reader will soon realize that he's been led on by a silly question. One can startle with a provocative opening statement like "Faith is a coma that keeps the spirit dead," but if what follows is the narrative complaint by a faithful speaker about his faithless lover, the reader may decide that an interesting generalization has lured him into hearing about a private peeve.

Some good beginnings seem obvious choices—*I saw a dimpled spider, fat and white* (p. 41). The idea for Robert Frost's "Design" probably started with the observation, and he starts the poem by telling about it. The three adjectives are arresting because they are unusual ones for a spider, and they are appropriate in hinting at the curious amalgam of innocence and evil that pervades the poem. The strength of the beginning lies in its vocabulary. Other good beginnings are more surprising—*That is no country for old men* (p. 117). For this poem, Yeats could have selected a particular detail from the first stanza as his opening line or have placed himself as arriving at Byzantium, as he does in line 16. His choice, undoubtedly the result of long consideration, is both arresting and appropriate. The reader wants to know what country is spoken of and what that firm statement means. And he is soon told these things, and told much more as well. Here the strength of the beginning lies in the assertion that the opening line makes.

Ending a poem is as difficult as beginning. The end, too, is a section where the risk of extra, pale verbiage is great, often brought on by a poet's imagined need to provide a concluding generalization or a denouement with less tension than the high point of the poem. Most good endings are not slopes of diminishing interest. They add something new and exciting to the poem, either an idea or synthesis not presented earlier or a summary in new, forceful language of what has been said earlier.

The value of a strong ending is well illustrated in the two versions of James Joyce's poems, "Ruminants" and "Tilly," on p. 142. The first version has an ending that seems to trail off weakly:

> When the herd too is asleep
> And the door made fast.

There is nothing really wrong with these lines, except that they lack the kind of weight in thoughts and words that would make the poem's conclusion memorable. A conspicuous improvement in the revised version is the concentration of heightened interest in the last two lines, where an unguessed speaker is suddenly revealed:

> I bleed by the black stream
> For my torn bough!

Good poems provide the best lessons about good endings. One can imagine the weaknesses that have been avoided in appreciating the strengths that have been attained. In the hands of a less skillful writer than Edwin Arlington Robinson, "Richard Cory" (p. 78) might have had an additional stanza to recapitulate the "moral" or, lacking that addendum, might have ended with a word less stunningly appropriate than *head,* a homely and mortal equivalent for *crown,* used earlier in the poem.

The importance of the final word demands that it be chosen with meticulous care. It is difficult to imagine a last word better for Stanley Kunitz's "Deciduous Branch" (p. 131) than *evergreen,* with its two meanings, both appropriate within the argument of the poem. The final *small* for "Design" seems equally exact, folding the poem's conclusion back upon its beginnings. In an earlier version (see p. 140), Frost used this last line: *Design, design! Do I use the word aright?* Although this poses the same question as *If design govern in a thing so small,* it is less interesting and graceful, partly because of *aright,* a strange word, old-fashioned or rural or in some way out of place, a verbal distraction that competes with the philosophic question that the last line raises.

All this is not to say that a good ending cannot recapitulate or summarize the idea of the poem. Such an ending, though, ought to be sufficiently distinctive to make the summing up seem worthwhile. In the last stanza of "Ars Poetica," MacLeish restates in a more general way what the preceding stanzas have argued:

> A poem should not mean
> But be.

Who can complain of repetitiveness, though, when so much is said so succinctly in words that stay lodged in the mind? The last stanza of "Pigeon Woman" (p. 4) is, in effect, a résumé of all the poem's action. But it allows for a close contrast between *lake of love* and *flints of love,* the states of the pigeons advancing and retreating, that makes the summary interesting and important. To end with an emphatic impression is part of the design of a good poem. Whether that emphasis should be principally linguistic or ideological or should be a balance of the two is one of the poet's major decisions.

Journal Projects

60. Look again at your poem that explains an abstraction through a series of metaphors and/or similes (Project #41). What determines the order of their arrangement? Have you made the best choices for beginning and ending the poem?

61. In Project #19, you devised two rhyming lines for a villanelle. Do you now consider the first to be an effective beginning? Would the two together provide a strong closing for the poem? If you are pleased with these two lines, work further on the poem.

62. Experiment with your persuasive poem in free verse (Projects #7, #16, #24, #30, #35, #46, #47, #52, #57), beginning it in different places. Do any of these new beginnings seem stronger than your earlier choices?

63. Return to your sonnet (Projects #12, #24, #30, #34, #46, #47, #55) to consider its beginning and its ending. Of the three examples used for the quatrains, have you begun with the one best suited to opening the poem? Does the summarizing couplet use an effective vocabulary? Is the generalization it makes interesting?

NAMING THE POEM

Naming a poem is, in many respects, like naming a baby. Sometimes the name chosen represents the poet's or parent's deliberate selection at an early phase of gestation. Sometimes it is a last-minute, panicky decision when the poem is ready for publication or the child for baptism. The name may be intended to honor a person or to commemorate an occasion. Or it may reflect the namer's personal whim or preference. Bestowing a name is an act of magic, an effort to give reality to some hope or wish that may or may not be fulfilled in the child or in the poem. There are girls called Joy who tyrannize over the nursery or the dinner table with sulks and snarls, and boys called Alexander who grow up to be weak, pale, and indolent. Poems, too, can fail to fulfill the promise expressed in their titles. Whatever the quality of the name—suitable or inappropriate, plain or elaborate, long or short, melodious or rasping, conventional or bizarre—it sticks fast to what it labels and usually remains the dominant identifier for a lifetime.

Many new poets send their poems out into the world without titles, and this omission often seems unfortunate. Although no title is better than a bad one, the unnamed poem labors under some of the disadvantages that would plague an unnamed person. One wonders why the poet has failed to name his poem —lack of confidence, laziness, indecision, a wish to be mysteri-

ous, possibly his own uncertainty about what the poem means?
Most writers hope that their poems will be read and remembered and referred to. But it is more difficult to recall or to cite
as an example the poem that has no name. If the work is as
distinguished as a sonnet by Shakespeare, or a lyric by Emily
Dickinson, the first line may become the means of identification. But most new poets cannot expect to make so indelible an
impression. Some authors, aware of the need to identify a poem
but reluctant to give it a significant name, adopt a mechanical
label; but calling a poem "Sonnet" or "Opus IV" is not usually
an effective solution. Robert Francis could have called his poem
(p. 53) merely "Sestina," but he would have lost that extra
identification and the suggested double meaning that "Hallelujah: A Sestina" makes possible.

There are some instances where the absence of a title is suitable, or is, at least, no disadvantage. A poem that is very short
—a couplet, a quatrain, a *haiku,* a limerick, for example—may
look top-heavy with any but the briefest title and may seem
better with no title at all. If the meaning is to emerge only as
the reader moves through the poem, as in a piece of found poetry or concrete poetry, a title may spoil the effect by revealing
information in advance. Had E. E. Cummings given a title to
his poem about fog, the reader would be deprived of some of
the aesthetic and intellectual satisfaction of puzzling out the
meaning from the text. For most poems, though, a title provides
a useful identifying label and, in many cases, it also confers
other values.

Some kinds of titles ought to be avoided in all but the exceptional instance. First, the title that vaguely describes the nature (as opposed to the subject) of the poem: "Random
Thoughts," "A Reverie," or "Fragment" serve only to notify
the reader that what will follow is probably a tentative draft
that the author holds in low esteem. Second, the hardy-peren-
nial title that has been used and reused through the centuries—

"Spring," "Lament" (unless, of course, one can write a "Lament" like Dylan Thomas's!), "What Is Life?", "Love Poem." More distinctive but somewhat chilling is the didactic title that openly threatens the reader with instruction—"Make the Most of Each Morning," "Grief Will Fade With Time," "The Path to Happiness." The too-cute, too-clever title is another familiar blunder; a comic pun, a current colloquialism, an absurd allusion that might be a good title for light verse is usually a deceptive distraction before an emotional and serious poem. Finally, there is the mystery title, often stunningly unique and esoteric, sometimes in Latin or Greek, that seems to have no connection with the poem itself, as though daring the reader to fathom some hidden purpose.

Fortunately, there are just as many ways of naming a poem that are useful and appropriate. And the process of considering a poem's title offers excellent opportunities to review and reassess the whole poem. Structurally, the relationship between title and poem can take one of two forms. The title can be separate and distinct from the text, or it can be the first word, phrase, or line of the poem. Most of the poems included in this book have separate titles. A reader makes a long pause after the title, somewhat longer than the pause between end-stopped stanzas, then proceeds with the poem itself. Only George Starbuck's double-dactyl poem "Said" (p. 94) has a title that runs directly into the text. Dylan Thomas could have chosen to make the first line of "Do Not Go Gentle Into That Good Night" serve simultaneously as the title, but apparently chose to repeat. Which structure the poet elects will depend on his own inclinations and on the poem. The separate title offers a greater variety of possibilities. But the poet who is unable to devise a separate title and whose poem begins with words sufficiently important to stand as a label may choose the run-in structure.

The title that is separate can have various thematic relationships to the poem it names. The simplest kind merely announces the topic evident in the poem itself—"Pigeon Woman," "The Kraken," "Sailing to Byzantium," "The Silver Swan." These are like the titles of such paintings as Rembrandt's "The Mill." One could perfectly well understand poem or picture without the name; it is a neat, accurate label without surprises. One should remember, however, that a topic label does not necessarily designate the real subject of its poem. The subject of "The Silver Swan" would more properly be "disillusionment" or "resignation," not essentially associated with a real swan at all, any more than "Sailing to Byzantium" is associated with an ocean voyage. Some titles, instead of focusing on the poem's topic, are made up of a critical word or group of words from the poem. Maxine Kumin's "Lately, at Night" (p. 59), for example, takes words from the first lines and puts them together, and the words give her poem an appropriate temporal reference.

A title can go farther in attempting to summarize the meaning of the poem, to give a general distillation of what it is about. In "Ars Poetica" (p. 7), MacLeish announces that the principles developed in the text are all to be considered as parts of the art of poetry. Robert Herrick's "Delight in Disorder" (p. 26) summarizes the theme for which the several couplets offer specific illustrations. Robert Frost's "Design" (p. 41) alerts the reader to the significance of the poem.

All of the titles mentioned so far are by nature redundant, that is, usefully repetitive. They emphasize an element contained in the poem, but do not provide information that the reader needs in order to understand it. Some titles, though, contain words without which meaning would be diminished. Adelaide Crapsey's "On Seeing Weather-Beaten Trees" (p. 13) is a good example. There the title seems very long for a poem that consists of just one couplet. But that title provides essential information—the concrete picture with which *our living* is to be compared.

A title can identify the person or thing that the poem addresses, as in Marianne Moore's "To a Steam Roller" (p. 65) or Denise Levertov's "To The Snake" (p. 112). Or it can identify the speaker of the lines as in Sylvia Plath's "Mushrooms" (p. 113) or Howard Nemerov's "The Map-Maker on His Art" (p. 21). Some titles give extra information that is more subtle, not absolutely necessary to the poem's clarity, but contributing to a thorough appreciation. "Nude Descending a Staircase" (X. J. Kennedy, p. 14), for example, may be read simply as a topic title. But many readers will be reminded instantly of the painting with the same name. Since the words of the poem so suitably describe the motions and colors of the picture, the pleasure of reading is doubled because of the title's allusion. "American Primitive" (William Jay Smith, p. 79) makes a similar reliance upon allusion. One thinks of American paintings called "primitive," rather direct, amateur efforts to recapture a face or a scene, lacking the polish of more sophisticated treatments. And some may remember Grant Wood's "American Gothic," in which a realistic rural couple is posed to suggest a formal portrait. Sometimes a title provides a clue to the poet's attitude towards what he presents. "Coup de Grâce" (p. 128) indicates that A. D. Hope sees Red Riding Hood's triumph in terms of combat, as though she were an expert in arms, not the helpless heroine of the fairy tale.

There are no firm rules about how to discover the best title for a poem. Indeed, there may be two or three different titles that will serve a poem equally well. But a poet will find it useful to consider certain questions as he reviews his completed poem. If he gives it no title, he should be confident that this omission is purposeful. If he does give it a title, he should ask himself whether the title is clearly related to the poem, verbally, thematically, or in both ways. Is the title too long or too reminiscent of titles used before? Does it trick the reader into expecting something that the poem fails to yield? If the title contains information that is not repeated in the poem, is the information clear enough for the reader to make the necessary connection?

Finally, does the title attract attention? A poet needs to remember that his words, if they are published, will be exposed to three classes of readers—those who have a keen appetite for poetry and read all the poems they encounter, those who have an aversion to poetry and never read it at all, and those who will read on provided the title and the first line seem intriguing. In naming a poem, the poet need worry little about the first two categories, but his chances of involving readers of the third type are larger if he is careful about the name that introduces his work.

Journal Projects

64. For each of the following Project poems that you have completed, list three or four good titles, and then try to establish which is the most appropriate and the most interesting.

    a. "Eight O'Clock" as a descriptive poem (Projects #5, #37, #49).

    b. The sonnet (Projects #12, #24, #30, #34, #46, #47, #55, #63).

    c. The persuasive poem in free verse (Projects #7, #16, #24, #30, #35, #46, #47, #52, #57, #62).

    d. The triolet (Projects #18, #47).

    e. "Delight in Disorder" with a less formal vocabulary (Project #27).

    f. The abstraction explained through a series of metaphors and/or similes (Projects #41, #60).

    g. The poem dependent on one extended metaphor or simile (Projects #42, #47).

TESTING THE POEM
WITH AN AUDIENCE

Writing poetry is not a sociable pursuit. Whether the poet is alone or among others busy in their own ways, he works in a state of isolation. Even if he were willing to share the stages of his progress, it is doubtful that anyone would enjoy the experience. Watching a form emerge from the sculptor's block of stone or hearing a melody emerge from the composer's keyboard would be interesting observations for an outsider. But intruding where a poem is being written would only offer the chance to watch someone chewing his pencil, pacing up and down the room, talking to himself, scribbling and scratching out notes, or typing a dozen variations of the same line. Most poets don't seem to mind the solitary character of their working but are likely to feel cut off when there is no one to see or hear the finished poem. The painter can hang his canvas on his wall; the potter can pass the salad to guests in his own bowl; but the maker of a finished poem has no graceful way to give it exposure. Bringing out a page of poetry before a gathering of miscellaneous friends is likely to produce uneasy looks, some foot shuffling during the reading, and kind but rather hollow comment when the performance is over.

Yet it is valuable to the poet's own sense of himself and to the quality of his work to break through the vacuum seal that often surrounds him. To do this, he needs the company of those who share his interest. There are localities where there is no one at all, others where only one or two persons can be counted on for attention and responsible appraisal. The poet who lives in a university community or metropolitan area where there are numbers of poetry writers and readers is truly fortunate.

Wherever he is, a poet usually feels the need for some setting where he can observe the reactions of others to his work and get specific criticism from people who know something about contemporary poetry. There are various arrangements that meet these requirements. Some poets seem to work best with just one other person. The two meet regularly (or phone or write if they cannot meet), exchange poems-in-progress, and comment on what the other has written. Together they assess ideas, weigh alternate arrangements, hunt for improved expression, juggle lines until a poem seems to begin and end in the right place. Such symbiosis can be so valuable, so important, that it becomes a part of the poet's working pattern. Obviously, arrangements like this are not common. It is a rare occurrence when two poets with compatible writing standards and temperaments discover each other and are able to arrange continuing contact. A writer cannot plan to form such a working partnership. If it happens at all, it just happens.

Somewhat less intimate is the informal workshop whose members meet periodically to share some of their work and to exchange criticism. A practical plan is to have each member bring multiple copies of a poem to distribute. When his turn comes, his poem can be read silently by everyone, then he can read it aloud. If the group works well together, comments will follow the reading, and the poet may see possibilities for revision that he had not thought of alone. This arrangement succeeds only under certain conditions. First of all, the group must be of the right size: three is probably too few, since there will be meetings where at least one person is unable to bring a poem; with eight or more, criticism for any one poem must be cut off too quickly if the meeting is not to last beyond comfortable limits. Second, those participating should be roughly equal in poetic ability. If one member always limps along while the others make good progress, or if one consistently soars while the others walk, frustrations may develop and criticism will lose its usefulness. Finally, it is helpful for an established informal workshop to invite a visitor from time to time. He will bring in a fresh point of view, reduce the tendency for each member to fill a predictable role. His presence will also remind members that the short-cuts in communication that familiarity allows may also result in slovenly analysis.

Some places where there is a concentration of interest in new poetry have more formal workshops, set up by a university, an adult education center, or a regional poetry club. These groups are usually larger than the informal workshop, some with as many as thirty participants, and they typically meet with a leader. He organizes the distribution of poems, selects those that are to be discussed, suggests subjects or forms for working assignments, and monitors the discussion so that it does not become too digressive or fragmented. The formal workshop, with its wider spectrum of competence among members and its very limited time for dealing with any one member's work, may be less satisfying than the smaller, informal workshop. On the other hand, the advantages of capable leadership and organization and the opportunity for a novice to ease his way gently into the critical process may prove to be very valuable.

Whether informal or formal, the workshop setting involves some penalties. A poet, especially a beginning poet, may experience devastating embarrassment or pain in exposing his work to others and watching it being dissected and reassembled, sometimes with a cool violence. A poem is an extension of oneself, and implications that it is less than perfect can be as unpleasant as a personal slur. Habit makes the hurt quite bearable for most poets, and eventually the poet learns to distance himself from his poem enough so that he can concentrate on the commentary without becoming defensive. He is never obliged to act upon suggestions for change. Ultimately he has the choice of accepting or rejecting them. He will realize greatest value if he looks upon workshop comment as extra information that may prove to be illuminating, a bonus added by outsiders to his own assessments of his poem.

The workshop also involves conspicuous benefits. Regular meetings have a disciplinary value. Even a motivated poet goes through dry stretches when he can't seem to get ideas or work them out, and busy periods when other responsibilities keep him from his poetry. The deadline imposed by the meeting, the need to get a poem into reasonably good shape for distribution, gives him a fixed responsibility, in some ways a burden but also a wonderful excuse for neglecting other matters in favor of writing. The regular obligation often serves as a test of the poet's own attitude towards his work. Many people think they want to write poems. But when the opportunity becomes real and the vague wish is translated into a requirement, some of them discover that what they really want is to have written poems. If the process itself has no joy at all in it, one does better to abandon the effort, at least temporarily. The rewards for poetry, even good poetry, are not so remarkable as to justify work that is relentlessly dull or odious.

A poet who is unable to arrange any continuing setting in which to test his poems may find it useful to enroll in one of the conferences or workshops that meet during the summer months, some for a few days, some for a week or two, some for even longer periods. Although a short stretch in company with others who are trying to write poetry, with infusions of comment from an established poet of two, is probably not as helpful as the cumulative effect of regular criticism, it may be better than no criticism at all. It will at least dislodge the poet from his world of solitary work and bring his poems out of the desk drawer into the view of people who are ready to read them with interest.

Whenever or however a poet gets the chance to share a poem with colleagues, there are two procedures that may make the process more useful and more satisfying. If he has the option of reading his own poem aloud, it will probably be better understood. This is not always possible. Some settings call for readings by the group leader, by another poet, or by an actor. Though such readers may have elocutionary skills that surpass the poet's, his intimate knowledge of his work makes him better able to convey his feelings and attitude, to know where to stress a word or syllable, where to pause, where to speed up or slow down the reading. These nuances are usually more important than excellence in declamation. Furthermore, a writer whose poem is under consideration by a group should be prepared to take full and accurate notes of the discussion. One expects that he will always remember what has been said about his poem, but the excitement of the occasion may cause him to forget useful responses. Taking down everything that the group offers requires a fast pen, but such notes can be invaluable for later revisions.

There is no substitute for the benefits that competent, face-to-face criticism can offer the poet and his work. Here is the way one poem fared in an informal workshop, the give and take of criticism reproduced as accurately as memory and some rough notes will allow. The author, just a few days earlier, had returned from a routine errand to discover that her house had been robbed. She was less disturbed by the loss of property than by small evidences of a stranger's presence in her room and the feeling that her privacy and security were permanently impaired. She tried to express that feeling in a poem and, after three or four revisions, read it, still somewhat warm and raw, for colleagues, A, B, and C:

Robbery

There's a shadow on my mirror,
There are footsteps on my floor,
The hint of a hand's dampness
On the handle of my door.

My dresser fittings tumbled,
My violated shelf
Give evidence the house is shared
With a predatory self.

There was a long silence during which the listeners reread
the poem and began to formulate their suggestions. Then the
barrage of comment began.

A. There's something annoying about the third and fourth lines.
Too many *h*'s in *hint, hand's, handle*. Besides, *hand's* and *handle* sound repetitive.

B. I agree. I was thinking of the repetitions of *my*. Aren't they
overdone? And the first two lines start with *There*.

A. It's jingly.

C. I like the idea of the poem, the suggestion that a robbery is
somewhat like a sexual assault. But it needs sharpening. The
words aren't good enough for the idea.

POET: I was trying to achieve an ominous effect. Somehow repetition seems to me to generate an ominous feeling.

C. Wouldn't it be even more ominous, even spookier, if you didn't
make statements that sound so controlled? Couldn't you just
say *Shadow on my mirror* instead of *There's a shadow on my
mirror*?

B. That's a good idea. It would get rid of some of the repetitions.

POET: O.K. But it will change the meter slightly. Maybe I can do
it. How about:

Shadow on my mirror,
Footsteps on my floor,

> Hint of a hand's dampness
> On the handle of my door.

A. Actually, that seems a metrical improvement. But the sounds in the third and fourth lines are still bothering me.

POET: I wish I could get into the lines the actual feeling I had that the print of a hand was just then disappearing from the knob, as though the burglar had left only seconds ago. It's the immediacy I need. That awful suspicion that an intruding stranger had just slipped away.

B. You could help to get that feeling by changing the title. *Robbery* isn't specific. If you called the poem *After the Robbery*, the reader would get a time reference and might infer that the act of robbery had just been committed.

POET: That's good. I like that better. If I make those changes in the first stanza, I'll need to change the second in a comparable way. It would then read like this:

> Dresser fittings tumbled,
> Violated shelf.

A. You could use *A violated shelf*. That would sound less artificial.

B. Getting rid of those repetitions of *my* is a distinct improvement.

C. There's something awfully cold about the diction that seems to prevent feeling from coming through. *Give evidence* is courtroom talk. I don't like that at all.

POET: I'm not satisfied with it either, but I can't find a good synonym for *evidence* that isn't just as cold.

C. You could say *Are proof*, but that's still somewhat legal. How about *Testify?* No, how about simply *Report? Report the house is shared* sounds like a more active, a more vocal giving of evidence.

POET: I'm not sure. *Report* suggests newspapers or guns or other things. It may have too many different meanings.

C. But that could be an advantage here. The word sounds stark,

sharp, like a rifle's report, and that increases the sense of violence.

B. What do you mean by *predatory* exactly? Is that the best
word?

A. I hate the sound of it.

POET: Maybe not the best word. I want the idea of a malevolent
and dangerous other self, someone whose victim I am or could
be. The idea of piracy came to my mind, and I thought of
pirate self.

A. I don't like that. And the verb *pirating* sounds awkward.

B. *Brigand?* No, that's no better.

POET: I oughtn't interrupt this train of thought, but I have a
revision for the third line that will get rid of the *h*'s. How
about *Evaporating dampness?* Or is that too heavy a word? I
think I like it.

C. That's better.

B. It seems inconsistent for me now to suggest that you insert a
my. But I think you need it in next to the last line. It's important to say *my house. Report my house is shared.* Doesn't
that seem right?

POET: O.K. I really don't want *predatory.* The more I say it,
the worse it sounds.

C. *Pirate, brigand, outlaw, pilferer.* I don't like any of them.

POET: Thanks for all your suggestions. I guess we've taken
enough time over this poem. It's stronger now than it was
and, as I work on it, I may think of some further improvements.

C. *Marauder.* How about *marauder?*

A. You could say *marauding. With a marauding self.* Metrically
it's good.

POET: Maybe. Let me think about it later.

Spontaneous and jumbled as these suggestions were, the author used almost all of them in her revision and made two further changes of her own. Length, stanza shape, rhyme pattern
remained the same as they had originally been. So did the in-

tention, the point of view, and the feeling of the poem. Changes in vocabulary and syntax, though, made the whole poem more compact and more forceful. Here is the way it looks now:

After the Robbery

Shadow on my mirror,
Footstep on my floor,
Evaporating dampness
On the handle of my door.

Dresser fittings fondled,
A violated shelf
Report my house is shared
With a marauding self.

The poem still isn't good enough, but it has moved in the right direction.

Another poem passed through even greater changes after its exposure to the same workshop. The author, Ruth Whitman, said she was moved to write the poem by a news item early in 1968—the fatal burning of three astronauts in their space vehicle at a Cape Kennedy work site. Newspaper coverage of this terrible event included photographs of the three men, notably one of E. H. White during the walk he had made in space a few years earlier. Ruth Whitman's original idea was to make an arrangement of alternate short lines that would simulate the funeral hieroglyphs on an Egyptian tomb; she wished to use the shape of the text to help make the meaning of the poem. This is how her poem looked:

Hieroglyphs for a Dead Astronaut

Reading you frontwards
               over your shoulder I see
The wornout earth
               like a teardrop shimmering

You loom out in a closeup
                              grinning foolishly
But your shoulderblade
                              blots out the map of Africa
Your earlobe lies
                              against the China sea
Tipsy in space
                              you knew you were history
Now I will give you
                              for burial toys a planet
To hold in each hand
                              I will paint an Egyptian eye
On your funeral ship
                              to read its way in the dark
Your sign like Orion
                              sprawled across the sky

The four other members of the workshop responded somewhat negatively to the poem, and made these criticisms.

A. *Reading you frontwards* is awkward, not very clear. (The
   author explained that this was the way the picture showed the
   astronaut in space.) It isn't an intelligible beginning. Is *frontwards* used correctly?
B. I find *Tipsy in space* too cute. It sounds a little like Emily
   Dickinson. Perhaps that should be changed.
C. I feel the same way about *you knew you were history*. There's
   something trite, too pat, about it.
D. The plan for simulating hieroglyphs does not really succeed.
   In the hieroglyph columns, each picture is an image. Here,
   each half line represents not an image but a verbal phrase.

The first three criticisms all have to do with language and
focus clearly upon individual words. The reference to Emily
Dickinson points up one important value that a poet can realize
from a workshop reading. He may have failed to notice that

some expression he has used suggests another poet. If outsiders listen, the chances of detecting a likeness are increased. The last criticism, in questioning the basic plan of the poem, must have given the poet the most trouble; her original idea, the way she had started, was, this critic suggested, possibly the wrong start. It is relatively easy to tinker with individual words and lines, but replanning the whole poem requires more courage, great effort, and new insight.

Ruth Whitman took the poem home, together with notes of her critics' suggestions. She revised the poem, then revised it several more times. Eventually, she abandoned the idea of hieroglyphs and decided to write the poem straight. Her final version, published in a series of short vignettes of disaster called "Public Images," which appeared in her collection *The Marriage Wig,* incorporated all of the workshop criticism except for keeping *tipsy in space,* which she judged to be appropriate. Here is the poem as it ultimately appeared:

THE LATE ASTRONAUT IN THE BOSTON GLOBE
grins foolishly at the unmanned
camera. Behind him
the earthglobe dangles.
His shoulderblade
blots out the map of Africa,
his earlobe overcomes
the China sea.
We've caught him,
tipsy in space,
walking nowhere.

Let's give him
burial toys—
two planets,
one for each hand,
let's paint
an Egyptian eye

> to steer his ship
> as he passes
> our old sky.

—Ruth Whitman (1922–   )

Epilogue

Typically, an epilogue "wraps up" the text it follows, and the reader feels that he has arrived at some final stage. Those who have worked through this book will face this epilogue without such a sense of completion. Learning about writing poems is a continuing process. The preceding sections, for practical purposes of order and communication, have reduced a long pursuit to the dimensions of a tidy package, and the Journal Projects have offered only signposts towards some of the directions in which a poet can move. Having come to the end of the book, the prospective poet may be just at the point of making his own beginning. This, then, is really a prologue.

Some writers will have worked enough on one or more of the Journal Projects so that they have poems that look viable enough to meet an audience or an editor. But others may find themselves with a collection of rough notes and not a single "finished" poem. This is no cause for discouragement. The Projects are exercises like piano scales and drawing-class assignments; under fortunate conditions, they may develop into finished pieces during practice, but more often they are the useful and necessary precursors to more accomplished work. Poets should keep their purpose firm, realizing that the Projects with which they are unsatisfied are really poems still in progress.

Of greater importance to the new poet are the attitudes towards his work that this book has tried to encourage: a respect for planning that is flexible enough to include the flash of inspiration, the thrust towards originality, or a change of direction; a recognition that, in a good poem, no single word is an automatic choice that can escape careful attention; and an acceptance of continuous evaluation and the willingness to revise again and again as essential parts of the process of writing a poem.

GLOSSARY

 *GLOSSARY*

Explanations of terms in this list have been phrased so as to make them especially helpful to writers of poetry. Some will, therefore, differ in style of definition, emphasis, and completeness from explanations for the same terms in books directed to readers and critics of poetry.

ALLEGORY   An extended metaphor encompassing events, in which actions, characters, and settings are intended as the non-literal equivalents of literal meanings.

ALLITERATION   Repetition of consonant sounds preceding stressed vowel sounds, as in *sugar/shadow/ shell*.

ALLUSION   In literature, the mention or suggestion of something from myth, legend, history, fiction, the arts, or current affairs not essentially part of the work. Allusion enables a writer to suggest briefly a motif, story, or personality for which the reader will have a body of associations in his stored knowledge.

ANAPEST   See METRIC FEET.

APOSTROPHE   Direct address for rhetorical or emotional

effect to someone or something who obviously cannot receive the message: to an inanimate object; to an abstraction; to an animal or plant; to a person who is dead or otherwise removed from the possibility of communication.

APPROXIMATE RHYME

Same as SLANT RHYME, *q.v.*

ASSONANCE

Repetition of stressed vowel sounds, as in *clothe/foam/doe.*

ATTITUDE

As used here, the poet's feelings towards his reader or audience as revealed in the tone of the poem.

BALLAD STANZA

The four-line stanza of alternating iambic tetrameter and iambic trimeter lines, rhyming *abcb,* frequently used for popular ballads.

BLANK VERSE

Unrhymed iambic pentameter lines.

CAESURA

A pause within a line of poetry, often, though not always, indicated by a mark of punctuation. The pause does not affect the metrical count. Such a pause in the middle of a line allows the poet to vary the pace and rhythm.

CLICHÉ

A word, phrase or longer expression that has become stale through excessive use. A cliché can be a literal expression, e.g. *a viable alternative, He's all boy,* or an overworked piece of figurative language, e.g. *Travel will widen your horizons, Mother Nature, silent as the tomb.*

CLOSED COUPLET

See COUPLET.

CONCRETE POEM

A poem that uses the arrangement of type

and other symbols to help make the poem's meaning. See also SHAPED POEM.

CONFESSIONAL POEM   A first-person, autobiographical poem in which the author's subject material is his own history, emotional state, and psychological configuration, and which includes some measure of detailed self-revelation.

CONNOTATION   The attitudinal values and other subtle meanings that adhere to a word. Some words have connotative quality that is general for everyone in the same culture; e.g., *healthy,* a word with positive value. Others may have private connotations for individual readers, e.g. *mother, work, black, white,* etc.

CONSONANCE   Repetition of consonant sounds following stressed vowel sounds, e.g. *give/arrive/of.*

COUPLET   A poem of two lines. Or a pair of rhyming lines, of any length or mixed lengths, used as a separate stanza, as part of a longer stanza, or as the unit of a poem in running form. A CLOSED COUPLET encloses a complete segment of an idea and ends with a mark of punctuation, signifying a pause in reading. An OPEN COUPLET runs directly into the next line. The effect of the closed couplet is crisp and organized; of the open couplet, expansive and relaxed. A HEROIC COUPLET is a pair of rhyming iambic-pentameter lines.

CURTAL SONNET   A term devised by Gerard Manley Hopkins to describe a shortened sonnet form that he occasionally used, having a six-line "octave" and a four-and-a-half-line "sestet."

DACTYL   See METRIC FEET.

DENOTATION   The precise meaning of a word without
                          overtones of feeling or value (connota-
                          tions). Of the three words, *child, tot,* and
                          brat, child is denotative, whereas *tot* has
                          positive connotations and *brat* negative
                          connotations.

DESCRIPTIVE POEM   A poem whose principal emphasis is upon
                          making clear a scene, an object, a person-
                          ality, or a feeling through the use of de-
                          tails.

DIMETER   A two-foot line. See LINE.

DOUBLE RHYME   Same as FEMININE RHYME, *q.v.*

ELEGIAC QUATRAIN   A four-line, iambic-pentameter stanza,
                          rhyming *abab*. Also called the HEROIC
                          QUATRAIN.

END RHYME   See RHYME.

END-STOPPED LINE   A line of poetry at the end of which the
                          reader is meant to pause, to signify a com-
                          pleted sentence, clause, or phrase. In tradi-
                          tional poetry, this is indicated by a mark of
                          punctuation. In some modern poetry that
                          is less punctuated, the pause may be dic-
                          tated by sense meaning alone.

ENGLISH SONNET   See SONNET.

ENJAMBMENT   See RUN-ON LINE.

EXACT RHYME   Same as PERFECT RHYME, *q.v.*

FEELING   As used here, the emotional response the
                          poet has to his subject or the response of
                          the reader to the whole poem.

FEMININE ENDING   The ending of a line of poetry with an

	unaccented syllable, usually an extra syllable added to an iambic or anapestic line. Also called a WEAK ENDING.
FEMININE RHYME	Repetition of stressed vowel sounds and consonants followed by identical unstressed syllables, as in *crazy/daisy*. Also called DOUBLE RHYME.
FIGURATIVE LANGUAGE	Expressions that are not literally true but that allow a poet to convey feelings and other nuances of meaning by making unusual associations. See also ALLEGORY, ALLUSION, IRONY, METAPHOR, OVERSTATEMENT, OXYMORON, PARADOX, PERSONIFICATION, PUN, SIMILE, SYMBOL, and UNDERSTATEMENT.
FIGURE OF SPEECH	Any one of various devices that express what is not literally true for the purpose of conveying feeling or other nuances of meaning. Also, any example of such a device. See also, FIGURATIVE LANGUAGE.
FOUND POEM	A formal or, more frequently, free-verse poem made up from a prose sequence not originally intended to have poetic value.
FREE VERSE	Poetry without predictable patterns of rhythm, rhyme, length of line, syllabic count, or length of stanza.
HAIKU	An old Japanese poetic form of three lines with five, seven, and five syllables respectively, using an image to suggest a season and to evoke a mood. Also simulations of this form in other languages.
HALF RHYME	Same as SLANT RHYME, *q.v.*
HEPTAMETER	A seven-foot line. See LINE.

HEROIC COUPLET	See COUPLET.
HEROIC QUATRAIN	See ELEGIAC QUATRAIN.
HEXAMETER	A six-foot line. See LINE.
HYPERBOLE	See OVERSTATEMENT.
IAMB	See METRIC FEET.
IMAGE	In poetry, an expression that suggests or conveys a sense impression. An image can be literal, e.g. *the blue and swirling sea,* or incorporated into a figure of speech, e.g. *leaping and devouring flames.*
IMPERFECT RHYME	Same as SLANT RHYME, *q.v.*
INTERNAL RHYME	See RHYME.
INVOCATION	Direct address to a deity, saint, or other supernatural agency who is presumed to be capable of giving assistance or at least of listening.
IRONY	A discrepancy that focuses upon the gap between the reality and its expression or anticipation. VERBAL IRONY is the saying of one thing while meaning another, usually just the opposite, e.g. *This is a fine state of affairs* for *This is a terrible situation.* DRAMATIC IRONY is the discrepancy between the limited knowledge of a character in a play, story, or poem and the larger knowledge of the audience or reader. IRONY OF SITUATION is the discrepancy between the way events turn out and the way they might normally have been expected to turn out.
ITALIAN SONNET	See SONNET.

LIGHT VERSE	Good-humored, witty poetry, designed primarily to amuse; usually written in a set pattern, often using clever rhymes. The subjects of light verse may be trivial, or they may be serious but treated in a light-hearted manner.
LIMERICK	A five-line jingle, where the first, second, and fifth lines have three stresses each and rhyme with each other, and the third and fourth lines have two stresses each and rhyme with each other, the material trivial and the effect cleverly humorous.
LINE	In poetry, whatever the author designates as belonging on one line, regardless of whether the printer can actually fit it into one line of type. Metrical lines vary in length and are named for the number of feet they contain:

> MONOMETER = one foot
> DIMETER = two feet
> TRIMETER = three feet
> TETRAMETER = four feet
> PENTAMETER = five feet
> HEXAMETER = six feet
> HEPTAMETER = seven feet
> OCTAMETER = eight feet

The first and the last two of these are rare in English poetry.

MASCULINE ENDING	The ending of a line of poetry with an accented syllable.
MASCULINE RHYME	Stressed, final syllables that are identical in respect to both assonance and consonance, as in *bone/moan*. Also called SINGLE RHYME.

METAPHOR — An implicit comparison between two dissimilar things. The metaphor can be constructed like an equation, e.g. *Sleep is a little death,* or submerged in some expression that does not use the verb "to be," e.g. *sleep's taste of mortality, buried in sleep, funereal sleep, dead asleep.*

METRIC FEET — Groups of two or three syllables that are the components of metrical lines. Metric feet are named according to their arrangements of stressed and unstressed syllables:

IAMB = two syllables, unstressed/stressed, as in *correct*.

TROCHEE = two syllables, stressed/unstressed, as in *farmer*.

ANAPEST = three syllables, unstressed/unstressed/stressed, as in *indisposed*.

DACTYL = three syllables, stressed/unstressed/unstressed, as in *melody*.

SPONDEE = two syllables, stressed/stressed, as in *daybreak*.

METRIC STRESS — A pattern of stresses in poetry that is largely shaped by the recurrence of a particular metric foot.

MONOMETER — A one-foot line. See LINE.

NARRATIVE POEM — A poem whose principal emphasis is upon the recounting of an event or a series of events.

NEAR RHYME — Same as SLANT RHYME, *q.v.*

OBJECTIVE CORRELATIVE — A term invented by T. S. Eliot to describe something in the external world able to be apprehended by the senses that the poet chooses to represent some internal emotion or thought, and which will represent the same emotion or thought for the reader. (See p. 105).

OCCASIONAL POEM   A poem written to mark a particular event, usually one with public as well as personal significance.

OCTAMETER   An eight-foot line. See LINE.

OCTAVE   See SONNET.

OFF RHYME   Same as SLANT RHYME, *q.v.*

ONOMATOPOEIA   Imitation in a word's sound of the word's meaning, e.g. *bang, buzz, pitter-patter*.

OPEN COUPLET   See COUPLET.

OVERSTATEMENT   An expression that inflates the literal truth not to deceive the reader but to enhance intensity of feeling or to make an amusing exaggeration. Also called HYPERBOLE.

OXYMORON   A tight combination of opposites that literally would involve contradiction but that is figuratively effective, e.g. *sweet sorrow, fearful joy*.

PARADOX   An apparent contradiction that can be resolved by intellectual effort.

PATHETIC FALLACY   A term invented by John Ruskin to describe a partial personification in which some capacity for feeling is attributed to an inanimate object.

PENTAMETER   A five-foot line. See LINE.

PERFECT RHYME   Rhyme in which the final stressed syllables and any unstressed syllables that follow are identical in respect to both assonance and consonance, as in *oak/broke, surly/pearly, durable/curable*. Also called EXACT RHYME, TRUE RHYME, or, sometimes, simply RHYME.

PERSONIFICATION

The conferring of some human quality (appearance, will, feeling, etc.) upon something that is not human. Total personification occurs when a whole person is suggested, as in the figure of Justice holding the scales. Partial personification concentrates on one or a few details, as the face of a clock. See also PATHETIC FALLACY.

POETIC LICENSE

The privilege permitted to poets (and other artists) to violate a rule or custom or to ignore a reality for the purpose of achieving some aesthetic effect.

PUN

One sound (or two sounds that are almost alike) that has two distinct meanings, both somewhat appropriate to the context. A deliberate pun can be intended to have either an amusing or a serious effect.

QUATRAIN

A four-line poem. Or a four-line stanza using any metrical arrangement, usually, though not necessarily, incorporating a rhyme pattern. See also ELEGIAC QUATRAIN.

RHYME

Similarity of sound shared by two or more words. The similarity includes both assonance and consonance in PERFECT RHYME and either assonance or consonance in SLANT RHYME. END RHYME is the likeness of sounds at the ends of lines of poetry. INTERNAL RHYME is a likeness of sounds at least one of which is not at the end of the line.

RHYTHM
: A pattern of stressed and unstressed syllables that has enough repetition to be somewhat predictable.

RUNNING FORM
: A form for poetry of no set length, suitable for use without division into stanzas, e.g., blank verse or couplets.

RUN-ON LINE
: A line of poetry that ends without a pause and from which the reader continues directly into the next line. The run-on quality of a line is more technically called ENJAMBMENT.

SENSE STRESS
: In poetry, the stressing of syllables that would normally be stressed in prose without regard to any metric pattern.

SENTIMENT
: Feeling, a particular feeling, or the expression of feeling.

SENTIMENTALITY
: The excessive expression in over-familiar language of certain feelings, either sad or joyful.

SESTET
: See SONNET.

SESTINA
: A poem of thirty-nine lines, divided into six stanzas of six lines each and a final three-line stanza. There is no rhyme, but all lines end in one of six words, according to a set sequence. The final, short stanza contains all six words. See p. 53.

SHAPED POEM
: That kind of CONCRETE POEM in which lines are arranged in a shape related to the verbal meaning of the poem; for example, a poem about a star in the shape of a star.

SIMILE
: An explicit comparison, using *like, as, so,* comparative modifiers with *than,* etc., be-

tween two things that are essentially dissimilar, e.g. *Time is more precious than platinum, a flower like froth.*

SINGLE RHYME   See MASCULINE RHYME.

SLANT RHYME   As used here, a likeness of final consonant sounds following dissimilar vowel sounds, as in *cough/muff,* or a likeness of final stressed vowel sounds followed by dissimilar consonant sounds, as in *slope/moat.* Also often called APPROXIMATE RHYME, HALF RHYME, IMPERFECT RHYME, NEAR RHYME, or OFF RHYME. See also RHYME.

SONNET   A poem of fourteen iambic-pentameter lines incorporating a rhyme pattern. The ITALIAN SONNET is divided into an OCTAVE of eight lines, rhyming *abbaabba,* and a SESTET of six lines that, if the form is used strictly, have only two rhyming sounds and do not end with a couplet (*cdcdcd, cddcdc, cdccdc*). The form is written as one stanza or as two with a break after the eighth line. The ENGLISH SONNET is composed of three heroic quatrains and a couplet, so that the rhyme pattern is *ababcdcdefefgg.* The form is usually written as one stanza, but sometimes is cast into two, three, or four stanzas. In practice, there are many variations of both forms and mixtures of the two.

SPONDEE   See METRIC FEET.

SPRUNG RHYTHM   A term devised by Gerard Manley Hopkins to describe poetry in which rhythm is determined according to the number of stresses or beats to the line, regardless of what pauses or how many unstressed syllables separate the beats.

STANZA   Two or more lines of poetry set off together in a poetic paragraph, typically used to describe such a paragraph when it is part of a longer poem.

SUBJECT   In a poem, the topic as specially perceived by the poet, as interpreted through his feelings, and as expanded in significance.

SYLLABIC POEM   A poem whose form is determined by the numbers of syllables in the lines. Syllables are read with sense stress rather than metric stress, and there is no necessary pattern of stresses.

SYMBOL   An image with literal and concrete meaning that suggests other figurative, sometimes abstract, appropriate meanings. A CONVENTIONAL SYMBOL is one with associations established by custom and understood by all members of the same culture, e.g., the White House or a handshake. A NATURAL SYMBOL is invented by the poet but seems obviously appropriate for the meaning it suggests, e.g., a flame to signify love or inspiration. A UNIQUE SYMBOL is also invented by the poet but is more difficult and surprising, e.g., a television screen to signify spying or surveillance.

TERCET   Same as TRIPLET, *q.v.*

TETRAMETER   A four-foot line. See LINE.

TONE   As used here, the expression of a poet's attitude towards his reader or audience in a particular poem, as admiring, scornful,

teasing, condescending, etc. Many poems
have the rather neutral tone that results
when the author considers the reader to be
someone like himself.

TOPIC

Of a poem, the subject at its simplest level,
the kernel around which feeling and significance accumulate to make the larger subject.

TOPICAL POEM

A poem that comments on an immediate
event or situation that has public as well
as personal significance, as on a news item
or a current social condition.

TRIMETER

A three-foot line. See LINE.

TRIOLET

A poem of eight lines, where the first,
fourth, and seventh are identical, and the
second and eighth are also identical. The
third and fifth lines must rhyme with the
first, and the sixth line with the second.
See p. 51.

TRIPLE RHYME

Stressed syllables that are identical in assonance and consonance and followed by
pairs of identical unstressed syllables, as in
beautiful/dutiful.

TRIPLET

A three-line poem. Or a three-line stanza
in which two or three of the lines rhyme.
The term TERCET is sometimes used inter-
changeably with triplet. Some critics, however, use triplet to designate a stanza where
all three lines rhyme with each other, and
tercet for a stanza where only two rhyme
or where the three lines are linked to other
stanzas through rhyme.

TROCHEE

See METRIC FEET.

TRUE RHYME   Same as PERFECT RHYME, *q.v.*

UNDERSTATEMENT   An expression that deflates and diminishes the literal truth not to deceive the reader but to indicate restraint or to provide a bitter, absurd, or amusing contrast.

VILLANELLE   A poem of nineteen lines, divided into five triplets and a final quatrain stanza. The first line is repeated as the sixth, twelfth, and eighteenth lines. The third line is repeated as the ninth, fifteenth, and nineteenth lines. The first and third lines rhyme and their rhyme is repeated in the fourth, seventh, tenth, thirteenth, and sixteenth lines. All other lines end in a single rhyming sound. See p. 52.

WEAK ENDING   See FEMININE ENDING.